RELIGION:
OUT
OR
WAY
OUT

WILL OURSLER

RELIGION: OUT or WAY OUT

WILL OURSLER

A GINIGER BOOK
Published in Association with
STACKPOLE BOOKS

To Jeannie Adele
who kissed me when we met

CONTENTS

A Manual of Church Planning. Expanded Service of the
Modern Church.

PREFACE

It is a new day, a new faith, a changing church.

It is a church that proclaims a need for relevance to an age that insists upon an increasing fusion of the sacred and secular. From ecumenism and "this worldliness" to new theologies and a spreading new "supernaturalism," now called parapsychology, unfolding developments in modern religion present disturbing issues to many millions of Christians. How far out can religion get?

This book is a front-line exploration of the current religious awakenings, the meanings and implications of what is happening, how these changing patterns of the church affect the rituals of worship, and the theological affirmations on which they are based.

Much of what is happening clearly reflects a resurgent vitality in the modern church. Challenging questions are raised by the church itself. They appear to add up to one basic, all-important issue: Is a new religious dimension emerging out of the ruins of outmoded and discarded literalisms and an almost morbid preoccupation with God's wrath and punishment rather than with His love and forgiveness?

Whether or not one agrees with the directions of this surging religious excitement is not the key. What is important is that believers and nonbelievers alike have a chance to examine, in all their many facets, the varieties of change that are taking place today in the patterns of organized belief and worship. This examination will determine the shape of religion in the years to come. Will it be "out?" Will it be "way out?"' Or what will it be?

To all who aided me in the research and gathering of a vast amount of material and interviews, I am deeply grateful. I want in particular to express my gratitude to my wife, Adelaide Burr Oursler, my chief researcher; to my "instant assistant," Wilma Dobie; to officials of the National Council of Churches; to Father William Walsh, director of the St. Ignatius Library in New York City; and to the officials of the major denominations who provided so much help in the preparation of this book. To all of these, as well as to the many other individuals who gave valued help to this work, but whose names would make too long a list for the space allotted here, my sincerest acknowledgment and deepest gratitude.

WILL OURSLER

CHAPTER I

THE MODERN CHURCH: NEW
FRONTIERS AND OLD TABOOS

The religious revolution of our times strikes at the very heart of
organized faith. It could make the church more meaningful than
ever before in its history. Or destroy religion as most of us know
it today.

This is the situation we face. Consider, as an instance, the
following:

"It is time for the church to do away, once and for all, with the
whole doctrine of original sin. Man was not born unregenerate
and evil; we sin in what we do to others, not in merely being
what we are. The whole Biblical account of creation is mythol-
ogy. Man and woman were not created on this earth in that
way."

This was no atheist sounding off against God. The words
were spoken to this writer by a learned and devout Episcopal
priest, the Rev. Joseph F. Fletcher, seminary professor in Cam-
bridge, Mass., former dean of St. Paul's Cathedral in Cincinnati,
Ohio, and author of several widely read books on situational
ethics and the so-called new morality.

1

The fact that a professor of theology could take such a position on one of the cornerstones of Christian dogma is a symbol, a clerical flag of new and controversial ideas.

There was a time when the lightning rod was considered sacrilegious. Sermons were preached by learned clergymen warning their parishioners to have nothing to do with Benjamin Franklin's insidious new invention. If it be God's will to strike your house with lightning, then let no human try to thwart it.

Every area of science, psychiatry and psychology, medicine, surgery and anesthesia, vaccination, technical advances across the centuries—all had first to struggle against theological denunciations.

Today the theological currents have dramatically reversed direction. Instead of challenging science and progress in the world, the church is challenging itself and its own beliefs.

Basic concepts long considered "absolutes" are undergoing reexamination—not only by those outside the church but often by those within. The Roman Catholic concept of celibacy is questioned, debated, sometimes denounced, by non-Catholics and Catholics, by members of the laity and by thousands of Roman Catholic priests. Vatican Council II was a landmark on the road to religious change. Traditional and liturgical procedures followed for centuries—violation of which constituted a sinful act—have been abandoned entirely or left to the option of the worshiper.

The scope of the changes covers the entire field of the church's concern. From spiritualism to social action, from picket-line priests to the laboratories of science and the shrines of miracles, religion roams the world of the material and that of the spirit with a wholly new zeal.

This is not to imply that all who interpret the Bible literally have surrendered to the newest crop of church liberals. It does mean that Biblical literalists are having a more difficult time defending positions that increasingly appear to be losing scientific and historical support. It means that even the most deep-dyed fundamentalist has begun to soft-pedal the more unlikely Biblical accounts. Jonah's three days in the belly of a fish can be given a variety of symbolic explanations without dwelling too heavily on exactly how such a thing could happen—or whether it happened at all.

The Baptists, as a church, still believe that baptism by total immersion is one essential for salvation. Yet many within their fold raise serious questions about all sacraments and ritual. One leading Baptist, Harvey Cox, author of *The Secular City,* suggests that perhaps we ought not to use the word "God" for twenty-five years because it has so many differing connotations that no one really knows what we mean by it. In another work, entitled *God's Revolution and Man's Responsibility* and developed out of a series of lectures, Cox discusses his own idea of baptism: "The next question to ask is whether our *form* of baptism is correct. . . . Is it possible that God may be suggesting to us today that we find a *new* way of saying the same thing, a new way of dramatically showing our solidarity with the suffering and the exploited of the world, a new way of declaring our participation in the ongoing crucifixion? . . ."[1]

In such questions we find a hint of the ferment in which religion finds itself. To some, this self-probing is a shaking off of the outmoded and no longer tenable, a return to the basic and eternal, which some churchmen sum up as *agape*—love itself, Christian love outgoing to all beings and all creation.

The church approaches new frontiers of mission not only of the physical world but also of the mental, emotional, and spiritual. The relationship of religion and healing is one of the most important areas in which new concepts are taking hold, in which new ideas embrace ancient beliefs, modified, reshaped to fit modern knowledge and modern belief. Religious healing began

---

[1] Harvey Cox, *God's Revolution and Man's Responsibility.* Valley Forge, Pa.: The Judson Press, 1965, p. 94.

with a priest and his prayers, and elsewhere with the tribal medicine man and his incantations. Later it moved away from religion and battled the church for a right to exist as a wholly secular discipline. Only in recent years has religious or "spiritual" healing again been accepted as part of the church's function.

The revival of religious healing in our churches is one of the new phenomena that run to the miraculous. Yet, with the exception of the Christian Scientists, the very clergymen who urge that we practice healing techniques in the church also urge the latest medical and psychological treatments with equal fervor.

Half a century past, so-called spiritual healing was denounced by medicine as fakery, hysteria, nonsense. Today, many in medicine work with ministers and priests; the role of religion and prayer at every level of medical treatment is growing.

Half a century ago also, the bright young sciences of psychiatry and psychology were locked in battle with the leaders of medicine and other sciences on one side, and under assault from clerical leaders of all faiths on the other. Churchmen warned from the pulpit that mankind's heritage of sin and guilt, dominant in the church of the Victorian age, was being derogated by the new psychological findings. Many feared that these alleged sciences were fraudulent, dangerous, and very probably a product of Satan, himself.

Gradually, the fledgling sciences began to obtain a foothold of acceptance in education and medicine; gradually also the church began to grasp the possibility that religion, rather than the new scientific techniques, would have to change, to adapt.

In changing, the church came to realize that these new fields of human activity and help were not necessarily enemies of God, but could be allies. Nor did their teachings necessarily eliminate man's responsibility to God, to his fellow man or to himself. As the new sciences began to be better understood, and their findings regarding the human mind began to be shaped into disciplined knowledge, many churches came to realize that at least some "absolutes" to which man had so firmly clung—including some relating to sexual taboos—were perhaps not absolutes at all. Frozen, unyielding moral codes of the past began to yield somewhat to the customs, needs, and realities of our own day.

At the same time, other currents of religion began moving away from the purely ethical or liturgical into areas of a revived involvement with virtually all aspects of the paranormal. These include not only parapsychology and extrasensory perception but also demonology, possession, spiritism, and a spreading revival of glossolalia, or "speaking in tongues."

It may be disconcerting, to one not familiar with this development, to sit in a church—in upper-class Westchester County, for example—and hear and see a congregation of well-dressed men and women mumbling meaningless words, gibberish sounds, as they pray: "Da, da, di di, duz mamamememo, ja ko dock doc, co, fi do kakak da. . . ."

Is this revival of deliberately cultivated "speaking in tongues" truly communication with God?

Such metaphysical frontiers are diverse, puzzling, and often suspect. The large numbers of churches and church members probing these fields make it increasingly imperative that objective investigators search out the validity or lack of it in these expanding areas of metaphysical concern.

That dangers of many sorts lurk in such areas is certain—if only in their obvious attraction to the mentally and emotionally unstable. Perilous or not, however, some modern clergymen are daring to probe this little used or understood "gift of the Holy Spirit."

The fact that modern man feels free to question, debate, and even discard sacred dogma, as well as to argue the pros and cons of the most ancient and sanctified practices, is one evidence of new awakening attitudes. The fact the Vatican Council has threshed out many such issues, with priests, bishops, and cardinals hotly engaged in vital debates on religious life, provides additional evidence.

Formerly, in most major denominations, individual members were simply forbidden to practice spiritualism or participate in séances or similar activities. Today many church members are demanding the right to explore any of these things. If organized religion itself hesitates, thousands of its adherents feel no such reluctance. Some—rightly or wrongly—investigate the latest "kick" in drugs. One minister told me, "I took a 'trip' with LSD and it was the most extraordinary event of my whole life."

Unfortunately, he gave no hint that he understood the tremendous danger that exists in even a single use of this drug. But his statement indicated the new daring—and the new peril—in much that is happening.

Also startling in the church have been changes in concepts of morality, sex and its customs. The whole conflict-ridden story of the would-be married Roman Catholic priesthood has become a front-page contest. Such issues as abortion, birth control in the Roman Catholic Church, premarital and extramarital sex relationships—all of these once settled and unquestionable areas have become scenes of open theological conflict.

Matching the spiritual conflict is the debate and revolution in ritual and liturgy of the churches in which such phases of worship hold high position. Despite Pope Paul's efforts to modernize the Roman Catholic Church and the language of the Mass, there are still traditionalists who insist on the changeless validity of the past. Nevertheless, the whole meaning and role of the liturgy in modern Catholic and Protestant churches has been under reexamination and renovation.

The word "liturgy" itself has deep meaning in worship. In ancient Greece, it meant a service that wealthy citizens of Athens were called on to perform for the state—at their own expense. Later, as the Christian Church took form and shape, the word came to mean the active participation of the congregation in the "work" of the church in the whole panorama of worship.

Developments in Catholic liturgy are matched by changes in the Protestant churches, in new forms, new music, in jazz singers at the altars of high churches on New York's Fifth Avenue, in folk-rock singers strumming fast-beat roads to God.

And the new liturgy of words and music is matched by new forms of architecture, new shapes, a new placement of the altar.

Some of these innovations in faith are a direct response to the charge of irrelevance that lay behind much of the abortive "God Is Dead" movement, both in England and in America. Religion, said the "God Is dead" people, was not meeting the needs of the world. Theology did not stand up to the new knowledge of science, archeology, space exploration; the church's teachings were too rooted in ancient guilt and hell-fire; its concern for individual salvation led it to excuse horrendous crimes against humanity and society. What many of the accusers failed to recognize is that religion was, has been, and is more than ever today, in a process of metamorphosis. Churches that once participated in the mockery of religion called the Scopes trial and its war against the teaching of evolution in the schools have long since shifted their ideas. Even the most fundamentally unchanged are grudgingly giving ground.

Thus we find the church moving in two directions—toward the intellectual, social-action church, participating in the world and its problems directly, on one side, and the new supernaturalistic movement on the other.

No unanimity is found among church leaders, however, as to how far the changes will or should go; some fear that if they continue in the direction of ever-widening permissiveness and latitude of interpretation, the church may become totally secularized and nonreligious, an organization that not only does not accept the Scriptures literally but in many instances does not even accept the existence of a Supreme Being.

The new role of liturgy and ritual, the new language of the Revised Standard Bible, the new Anglicized Mass of the Roman Catholics, the new, much-denounced jazz masses—all of these cause consternation and denunciation from the fundamentalists, the Pentecostals, the traditionalists.

Changes nonetheless have come. They will almost certainly continue to come in the years ahead. This appears to be the inexorable fact faced today by believers of every faith.

It appears also that some of the roads being explored by the churches go in divergent directions. What this can mean to all religion now and in the future is extremely significant.

Are the "way-out" developments merely sideshows on the mainstream of faith or are they symptomatic of a movement back to beliefs that large segments of the world today have totally rejected?

Or will the total renovation of the church in all its various phases, under the leadership of younger church intellectuals, prove to be the dominant, decisive factor in a modern restoration of meaningful religion?

Neither the new intellectuals nor the new supernaturalists in the church find themselves directly opposed to each other. Each is aware of his own need to reach out to new truth. It is a moment of change that holds the deepest import for religion and perhaps for all humanity.

THE HEALERS AND THE HEALED

Religion and healing have been companions across history. From the most primitive times, man has considered sickness and physical injury to have some relationship with the gods. But the modern church has added a third partner—the latest findings of medical science.

The partnership of church and healing practices has been an on-again-off-again story. By the mid-twentieth century, the spreading revival of metaphysical healing had become one of the thorny issues in the church. So-called "faith healing" has raised grave questions. Are the healings similar to the miracles of Christ happening in modern times? Should healing ministries be encouraged or even allowed by the church?

Or do such healing pastors revive false hopes, lead individuals to do themselves serious harm, possibly even cost them their lives?

Those who believe in religious healing point to the Scriptures themselves. Healing is cited in the New Testament as one of the gifts of the Holy Spirit. It was carried on by the disciples of Jesus.

Nor is there any record that it was forbidden to mankind in the future. The Presbyterian Church, in *The Relation of Christian Faith to Health,* explicitly points out: "The Church must not put limits on God's ability to heal by any means He chooses. In the light of contemporary medical, psychological and religious experience there is increased reason to affirm with Calvin: 'The Lord is undoubtedly present with his people to assist them in all ages; and, wherever it is necessary, he heals their diseases as much as he did in ancient times.' "[1]

Such therapy cuts across all religion; the church has been intimately a part of the healing process since before the dawn of Christianity.

Healing techniques and practice are not limited to Roman Catholic shrines or Christian Science practitioners. Virtually all denominations have some relationship to faith therapy. Major Protestant denominations have healing rituals and prayers, and many individual churches have regular healing services employing special techniques including the Eucharist and the laying on of hands by the pastor.

Some churches have come to acceptance of spiritual healing therapies very slowly. Often church authorities give support to such practices only with reluctance. Despite traditional shrines and healing centers in the Roman Catholic Church, for example, many priests and communicants regard the shrines as dubious at best—and possibly emotionally and physically dangerous.

Yet religion has—despite its alarms—swung back to its ancient participation in healing. In large measure its new role involves cooperation with medicine and psychiatry. But it also remains a role of faith, of prayer.

The Presbyterians present a dramatic case in point.

This church had been among the most disdainful of faith healing. One of its leading members wrote a book in the 1950's

---

[1] *The Relation of Christian Faith to Health.* Philadelphia, Pa.: The United Presbyterian Church in the United States of America, 1960, p. 40.

bitterly attacking so-called faith-healing cults. The emotionalism, the outward healing rituals, all were disturbing to Presbyterian practice and approach.

Yet, at the same time, Presbyterian leaders realized that the challenge of the healing movement from church members could not be ignored.

In 1956 the General Assembly of the United Presbyterian Church in the United States of America appointed a special committee to report on the whole relationship of "Christian faith and health." The reason cited for this appointment declared in part: "The genesis of this assignment by the General Assembly was a study made by the National Commission on Evangelism . . . . The Commision found that there had been a development in recent years of faith healing cults and of healing evangelists who, in the opinion of some, not only had put an over-emphasis on the physical body but also had appeared to use the power of God in a sensational way for self-glorification and publicity purposes. On the other hand, it found that there had been a growing conviction in many quarters that the relation of religious faith to health had been a neglected area in the pastoral ministry. Various communions among the more conservative Churches, both in this country and abroad, had undertaken to explore this whole area of the Church's concern. Many of our own pastors had expressed a desire for guidance in this matter. . . ."[2]

The committee's findings and recommendations, adopted four years later by the 172nd General Assembly, while still presenting a conservative approach, urged that all faithful Christians recognize that faith in God, and the love of God, play some part in healing. Discussing the methods of Jesus, the report declared:

"The healings of the New Testament are matters of vital relationship between God and man; their secret is not in the procedures. . . . What we learn from these records is that

---

[2] *The Relation of Christian Faith to Health.* Phadelphia, Pa.: The United Presbyterian Church in the United States of America, 1960, p. 3.

healing goes out from some who are in union with God and who are thereby sensitized to the needs of fellow human beings . . ."[3]

Affirming the value of prayer in healing, the Presbyterian report summed up its revised approach:

"The contemporary situation calls for the recognition of both the limits and the possibilities not only of established therapies, such as those approved in present day medical schools, but of new ones, such as the discipline of prayer. This is a time for exploration and experimentation in the religious dimension of healing. God has many therapies, and it is contrary to the spirit of science as well as to the faith of Christianity to absolutize any therapeutic methods."[4]

By the 1960's, numerous Catholic and virtually all Protestant churches were officially and unofficially involved to various degrees in religious therapy and its by-products—clinics, healing services, prayer groups devoted to individual cases including healing, and service by clergymen, physicians, and psychiatrists in counseling roles.

To understand the increasing influence on the church of modern religio-medical therapy, it can be helpful to examine briefly how this force emerged and from what wellsprings of organized belief and doubt.

The nineteenth century produced a strange ambivalence—an almost ruthless materialism on one side and flights of unfettered spiritual fancy and faith on the other. The second half of the century was, in fact, a period of shattering assaults on long-held beliefs. Darwin had planted his flag; a monkey's tail fluttered in the religious winds. The Biblical record was under assault and the "club sandwich" universe—"heaven and hell with a patty of earth between"—was being challenged.

---

[3] *Ibid.*, p. 20.
[4] *Ibid.*, pp. 40–41.

Psychology was barely starting. Freud had yet to evolve his theories. Geology, which was to open up millions upon millions of years of earth life, was still in unaccepted scientific infancy. The age projections of the geologists regarding the world's rocks and soil were greeted with derision by many fundamentalists.

Nevertheless, the forces of science, religion, and medicine as well as ordinary worshipers began testing the validity of old ideas against the startling revelations and implications of the "New Thought" era.

That Mary Baker Eddy's Christian Science led the way in this development cannot be questioned. Its teachings, however, were not only suspect as possible fraud but also ridiculed mercilessly, and those who followed its ideas were regarded as at least half out of their minds. How could a man who was sick be healed by repeating from the Christian Science textbook, *Science That Heals with Key to the Scriptures,* a few phrases like Mrs. Eddy's "scientific statement of being," which begins with the assertion that "there is no life, truth, substance, intelligence in matter, that all is infinite mind and its infinite manifestation . . ."

People could accept a Roman Catholic visionary saint such as Bernadette and her experience at Lourdes; they could accept the possibility of the miraculous even if some nonbelievers thought it was all either fraud or emotionalism. But such miraculous healings, others believed, existed only as part of the great, centuries-old pattern of Roman Catholic faith.

Christian Science threw away the religious medals, the anointing oils, the beads. It drew on other sources of faith. There was no statue before which the devout could kneel. Mrs. Eddy was insisting that you were not sick at all; that reality when understood had no place for sickness, pain, or suffering.

Orthodox churches, their oaken resistance gleaming from every pew, regarded most of this as nonsense. But their clergymen noted that people *were* apparently being healed. It could not all be self-delusion or self-deception. Some of the reports were too well substantiated. Some people—by nature or God or something—were being made well without benefit of medicine.

Out of this was to begin a reexamination by some of the most conservative religious bodies. The Episcopalian revival of religious healing began—as did Christian Science—in the Boston area. But whereas Christian Science set up its banners with a cry against the whole medical profession, the Episcopal movement went in exactly the opposite direction.

The Emmanuel Movement in the Episcopal Church was so named because its founder, the Rev. Dr. Elwood Worcester, was pastor of Emmanuel Church in the Boston area. The local press began to report healings at this church and refer to the Episcopal healing ministry as the "Emmanuel Movement." What had happened was that many of Dr. Worcester's parishioners began to ask searching questions about Christian Science. Episcopalians might not accept the principles of Mrs. Eddy, but the actual healings were something else. The more Dr. Worcester explored, the more convinced he became that a ministry of healing belonged in the church, working in cooperation with, rather than opposition to, the medical profession.

In 1966, Dr. Worcester, with another Episcopal minister, the Rev. Samuel McComb, and a physician-professor from Tufts Medical School, Dr. Isidor Corist, met to discuss how they could best cooperate in the cause of healing.

Out of the meeting came the church-clinic concept and the beginning of the idea of "total healing." Medical men and ministers worked side by side in the clinic started at Emmanuel; literally thousands of persons came to the meetings; illness and problems were brought to the joint medical-religious staff. The Emmanuel Movement set the pattern for other clinics in the Protestant Church, including the kind of clinic later established at New York's Marble Collegiate Church by Norman Vincent Peale.

A continuing—if unspectacular—concern with church healing marked the closing years of the old century and the opening of the new. But the end of World War I ushered in an era in which religion itself was no longer fashionable. The healing movement as such did not again emerge in any serious way until the years after World War II, when many of the new horizons of the church began to come into focus, and young men and clergymen returning from the war and graduating from seminaries opened up a whole new perspective.

Religious healing represented a complete break with the belief, largely a leftover from medieval thinking, that it is God who visits sickness upon us, for His own purposes. (Some early medieval monks called it rebellion to God's will even to see a doctor, to treat a sickness, to pray to be healed, or to seek to have someone else healed.) Most major religions, both in England and America, totally reject the notion that God brings evil or sickness upon us. It is rather we who, by our own deeds, bring it upon ourselves.

"Healing is an expression of God's saving love for man," the Lutherans declared in a 1966 statement, Christian Faith and the Ministry of Healing. "According to the witness of the Gospels, Christ healed out of mercy toward a sinful and suffering humanity, in the sure knowledge that it is God's will to deliver men from all kinds of evil. God acts in love."[5]

Lutheran religious therapy—and this is equally true in the Episcopal, Methodist, and Presbyterian churches—clings strongly to the principle of total healing. "Spiritual ill health," declares the report, "may affect man's physical well-being; or, conversely, . . . physical ill health may affect his spiritual condition. The whole man needs to be healed, or saved, if he is to be healed indeed."[6]

The Lutherans warn, however, against extravagant claims,

---

[5] Christian Faith and the Ministry of Healing. American Lutheran Church, July, 1965, p. 6.
[6] Ibid., p. 7.

against seeking to "manipulate the will of God" to heal. "The healing service must be so conducted as not to impugn the faith of such as are not healed. It cannot be taken for granted that it is the will of God to heal all who have faith to be healed, and that therefore the only reason why there is no healing is lack of faith in him who is sick."[7]

Attempts to explain failures as "the will of God" seem to be no more logical than to claim that God wanted the person sick in the first place. Is there not the possibility that other factors are involved, factors concerning the individual as a human being with human frailties and weaknesses that cannot be defined as sin or wickedness but can be blocking healing? This is a view held by many in the healing movement today.

There is the instance of the evangelist—now dead—who told a child with braces on her legs to take off the braces and walk across the stage to where he stood with arms outstretched. Bright-eyed, full of her belief, she did as he ordered, only to collapse and break her leg as she tried to take her first step.

The child might have been healed—or emotionalism might have carried her across the stage safely, as the healer perhaps had hoped.

But no one commands healing with a snap of his fingers. And no one has the right to risk the safety of a child merely in the hope of staging a spectacular act.

Quite the opposite is the approach of a famous Episcopalian healer, the Rev. Dr. Alfred W. Price of St. Stephen's Episcopal Church, one of the oldest houses of worship in Philadelphia. His healing services and lectures are devoid of emotionalism. He insists that those who come to him must also have medical treatment and spiritual counseling.

A tall former football player and U.S. Marine, Dr. Price has little time for the trivial, the cliché, the formalistic. A man of

---

[7] *Ibid.*, p. 14.

driving force, he seems to cut through all that would impede him with a compulsive need to help human beings in trouble, an irrepressible faith that God can, will, and does heal if we give him the chance, if we eliminate the negative forces in situations where we ourselves may be creating or sustaining the environment of antagonisms, hatreds, unreconciled conflicts.

Tens of thousands of people have come to this church since Dr. Price inaugurated the healing clinic and its services in 1954. They come from all parts of the country and the world. Every type of illness and every stage of its progress are represented. Many are not healed. Some find a kind of release even if physical healing does not come. But others are healed in this church by these prayers. Many are too sick to come themselves to St. Stephen's. Relatives come to pray for them, or their name is given to the group that prays in shifts around the clock; twenty-four hours of every day, some part of this group is at prayer. All who make up the prayer group have been healed themselves through prayer at St. Stephen's Church.

In addition to Presbyterian, Episcopal, Roman Catholic, and Lutheran churches, healing therapies and practices are found in Methodist, United Churches of Christ, Baptist, Evangelical and Reformed, and Pentacostal churches as well. In thousands of parishes and churches, healing services are held regularly without fanfare or extravagant claims.

Many clergymen fight against becoming involved in healing. A rather typical example is the Reverend Harry D. Robinson, Jr., pastor of the First Methodist Church, Mt. Vernon, N.Y. Earlier in his ministry he had a church in Bellmore, Long Island, New York. A member of his congregation was associate director of a group called The Laymen's Movement for Christian World, with headquarters at Wainwright House in Rye, New York. Wainwright House held frequent discussions of religious healing and other psychic phenomena, and the associate director tried to induce Dr. Robinson to attend some of these meetings. Totally uninterested, Dr. Robinson kept making excuses. Finally he did consent to attend a talk by a healer from Baltimore, Maryland.

Robinson later recalled: "My wife had been suffering acutely with bursitis in the shoulder for some time and had had extensive medical treatment including cortisone and other therapy. The doctors had decided that the only thing that might help was a difficult operation that involved scraping calcium from the socket of the bone.

"We listened to this remarkable Baltimore healer, Ambrose Worrall. At the close of his lecture we filed along with the rest of the audience to shake hands and say goodnight. When he came to my wife, he said, 'You were sitting there thinking if he can do all these things, why can't he fix my shoulder?' "

To Robinson and his wife the quiet statement was jolting. Worrall asked her to sit down, and he placed a hand on her shoulder—the affected shoulder, although she had not indicated which one it was. He closed his eyes, stood there a minute, then opened them and said to her: "There now, I think that will be better. Raise your arm."

Mrs. Robinson had been able to move her arm only an inch or two before this moment, and then only with intense pain. Now she lifted her arm with virtually no difficulty or pain. "We left with gratitude and amazement at what had happened," the Reverend Robinson stated. "Within a few hours my wife had no sensation of pain at all; her bursitis had disappeared completely. She has not had a recurrence since that night. That was approximately twelve years ago."

The healing of his wife by Worrall, who happened to be an engineer in a Baltimore aircraft company, made a profound change in the attitude of the Methodist minister. He began to study spiritual healing, the history, the facts, the theories, the techniques.

He attended other lectures and seminars at Wainwright and elsewhere. Gradually he began to understand that one did not need a charismatic gift. There were techniques of prayer, the laying on of hands, intercessory prayer for others, the power of the Eucharist. Psychic healing, pastoral counseling, and medicine were truly allies, he came to believe.

Out of these months of preparation, results began to come in his church to fill the needs of people who came to him. An elderly woman, a relative of a member of the church, had failing eyesight. Her letters to relatives were written in large, spidery handwriting. When the member presented her name, Dr. Robinson led prayers for her at public healing sessions. Over the weeks, the church member reported that the woman's handwriting was improving. Later word indicated that her eyesight had been restored to a remarkable degree.

A World War II veteran was a patient in a mental hospital; hope had virtually been given up for his recovery. An aunt of this veteran came to Dr. Robinson's healing services and prayed for her nephew. Word came of a dramatic change: He had inexplicably improved to such an extent that he was able to return home and soon afterward he obtained a job.

A young married woman, a member of the church choir, had been diagnosed as having cancer of the breast. The Methodist pastor stated of this case: "I met with the choir the day the diagnosis was made. There were, I believe, some thirty members in the choir and I asked that they all pray while I laid on hands—placing my hand on her shoulder and head. She went to Roosevelt Hospital twenty-four hours later . . . I waited throughout the day with her husband while she was in the operating theatre and the recovery room. All the tissue for analysis was examined and the biopsy showed it to be nonmalignant. That was about nine years ago. There has been no sign of cancer on repeated examinations . . ."

There is no great "promotional" campaign, no crutches on the wall, no whipped-up tent-show hysteria. Healing here is simply a part of the on-going functional role of faith.

What is significant is that this kind of pastorate is found today in hundreds of churches.

They are the symbol of a renewed concern in what was once, and has become again, an important but still controversial aspect of today's religion.

This concern is not limited to physical ailments. The church of our times has to deal with other needs, hungers, and hurts—including the confusions and frustrations that dwell sometimes not only in the body but also in the loneliness of the human mind.

THE CHURCH AND THE MIND

Modern sciences of the mind have not and in all likelihood never will destroy the Judaic-Christian doctrine that man's will is free, that he knows right from wrong and is responsible for his acts.

But these sciences are putting increasing limitations on the absolute character of the dogma of free will. There are compulsions, there are hidden factors little understood by the individual impelled to antisocial acts. There are causes that can be searched out—and removed—by psychological techniques.

Today's church has been challenged to use these disciplines as new God-given tools.

The advent of Sigmund Freud has been called the true beginning of modern psychiatry. It marks also, in the minds of many, the dawn of a new approach, a fresh look at the church, all churches, in the light of the Freudian view of man's existence.

The jolting fact of Freud was the beginning of warfare that still rages in some quarters. Those who defend the doctrine of original sin fall back on the ancient Biblical legends. The alleged fall of man is defined by the more enlightened in broad philo-

21

sophical rather than personal terms. We are guilty, these views assert, not as individuals but as part of our God-estranged humanity.

Man's evolving understanding of himself, his mind, and his guilt or innocence has not come easily; we are indeed only on the fringes of investigation and exploration of that realm. But no examination of what is happening in religion could make sense without a concern for the impact of the psychological sciences and the psychological needs of our times, particularly as they relate to faith.

It is tragic that development of psychiatric knowledge and understanding has taken so long; equally unfortunate has been the slowness of the process by which the church has accepted the reality of pyschological causes behind actions previously considered the work of the devil or of man's innate evil.

Before the nineteenth century, the mentally ill were treated with unbelievable inhumanity, although there were certain gradual improvements. Physicians such as Philippe Pinel in France and William Tuke in England began to alleviate some of the worst conditions and to treat the insane as patients rather than monsters. In America modern psychiatry began to take shape under the late-eighteenth-century leadership of Benjamin Rush, called the father of American psychiatry, whose book on diseases of the mind was for many years the only such work written by an American.

The revolutionary explorations and researches of Sigmund Freud, however, in the late nineteenth and early twentieth centuries, truly opened the doors. At the same time they presented religion with a direct assault on the doctrine of man's sinful nature. As Freud began to analyze the minds of his patients, he looked not for guilt to punish but for a cause to understand, to correct and, if possible, eliminate. Sex and sexual desires, he insisted, were not sinful per se; they were part of our normal impulses and drives in and out of marriage. Deeply hidden guilt feelings associated with sex, he asserted, were among the chief causes of disorders of the mind, the personality, the ego. In talks to medical groups, he declared that neurotic disorders were due exclusively to such causes and conflicts, often traceable to sexual episodes, frustrations, or excitations going back to childhood and early infancy.

At the same time, Freud began to develop techniques for exploring *terra incognita*—the secret places of the mind. This led to the development of his psychoanalytic techniques—the patient who talks and the doctor who listens, the probing journey into the self. The sense of guilt that is buried below a neurosis could be dealt with, Freud determined, once the causal forces were found and brought into the open.

Religious leaders in the late Victorian day saw in such theories the hand of Satan. Most medical authorities denounced and deplored Freud's ideas. But Freud was concerned with his own paths of truth.

He did have certain followers. One was Carl Gustaf Jung, a Swiss psychiatrist who ultimately broke with Freud on the view of sex as the total cause underlying the libido and the drives of the unconscious. Jung was much closer to the metaphysical; he wrote and spoke of the collective mind as a force, a cohesive god-force of collective thought to replace traditional deities. Unorthodox in almost all his views, Jung insisted that the religious experience did exist. In this sense he went beyond Freud. The grace of God, in Jung's words, can be found in the experience that helps you to make your life "healthier, more beautiful, more complete and more satisfactory to yourself and to those you love."

Alfred Adler, also a follower of Freud in the early Zurich era, represented a third force in modern psychiatry. If Freud was sex and Jung was closer to pristine psychic love, Adler was the social influence, the play of the group and the outside world upon the individual, the effect of social relationships, the personal interplay of emotions.

The theories of these men complemented and at times overlapped each other. The sexual, the broader cosmic pool of mind, the interaction of person to person and society to individual all played a part in the new understanding and psychological help for the individual.

Many clergymen closed their eyes and hoped that the disturbing new ideas would go away. They deplored attacks on traditional morality. They urged their congregations to stand firm. The public, however, including many churchgoers, found themselves accepting more and more of what the "mind merchants" were saying.

In a lecture some years ago on religion and psychic health, the Rev. George C. Anderson, founder (1954) and honorary president of the Academy of Religion and Mental Health, asserted that modern Christianity may be on the verge of theological changes as radical as those of the Protestant Reformation. "Ills of the body distort the mind," he told his listeners, "and ills of the mind distort the body. What a man believes about religion will depend on his emotional and psychological health. A pastor's knowledge of the body and mind of man is as important as the knowledge of his theology and even of God."

The age-old antagonism of religion and science was never more sharply delineated than in these opening skirmishes between church and psychiatry. But the thunder of pastors against Freud and his followers was an exercise in futility. The lonely, the rejected, the confused ran, walked, or stumbled into the offices of a new priesthood of the mind.

The war between the pulpit and the couch spluttered and flared and died in the onrush of the 1920's; few except the fundamentalists remained concerned about religious dogmas. The fantastic mockery called the Scopes trial did much to damage religion's modern image. The Thirties and Forties brought new patterns of unemployment, depression, hunger, New Dealism, a new radicalism and agnosticism, the rise of Hitler, the aggressions of Japan, and ultimately the second World War.

Out of this unleashed violence came the new world of people who had lived through horror of unprecedented scale, through postwar revelations of gas chambers and human slaughter by the millions—the most loathsome single crime in the history of man. All of this had happened; it was upon our shoulders, upon all who played some part, in America as everywhere in the world.

Psychiatrists did a rushing postwar business: The split atom had become a split world. Tensions left their invisible wounds in the American psyche, and the need for mental and emotional help increased daily. In the period of the Fifties virtually every pastor and church felt the pressure of people in trouble, people on the brink of breakdown, parents with children they could not control, a rash of new drugs and new addictions, alarming increases in all forms of crime, notably juvenile crime.

Out of this also came new techniques in modern pastoral counseling. The pastor was no longer merely a fund-raiser for postwar church buildings; too much of modern humanity was turning to the clergyman for help.

As pastors became more and more involved in individual counseling, delving into the deepest human problems, the need became obvious for real professional staff including psychiatrists and social workers, as well as standard admission, treatment, and follow-up procedures. Clinics and trained staff began to be shaped under the leadership of the pastor.

Exemplifying the high level of development that churches were to achieve is the Pastoral Counselling Center of the First Community Church, in Columbus, Ohio. Pastoral counseling with professional psychological guidance began in this church in 1957. Individuals from all over the area, including those who never went to church or never belonged to any, began to ask for help and guidance. A report on this extraordinary place of help and guidance, published in the church news bulletin, declared: "In February, 1946, the Pastoral Counselling Center was organized to deal more adequately with their problems and to bring to bear the healing disciplines of the community such as psychology, testing, psychiatry and social work as well as pastoral counselling. In May, 1966, it became the first such center to be accredited in the nation."[1]

Who comes to such a community center for help? They are people with problems that seem beyond them in some way, beyond their own control or help. The words clinic people hear most often are simply, "I need to talk with somebody." The report gave the following facts about who and what and how many these people are:

"A glance at the monthly reports so far this year reveals that once a month an average of 144 persons are seen for 271 appointments (1.9 appointments each).

"Of these 55 are men and 89 are women. Forty-one (29 percent) are members of First Community Church and 103 (71 percent) are non-members who have been referred by ministers, lawyers, and doctors.

"In addition eighty-three persons a month attend role-playing sessions. Forty-eight persons have attended the four role-play workshops held so far this year. Inclusion of these figures raises the average of contacts per month to 354.

"The appointment load in the Pastoral Counselling Center has increased each year since the Center opened. In 1964 there was an average of 159 appointments a month (excluding groups) and an average of 225 appointments a month in 1965 (excluding groups).

"The people who come to the Center are all ages and in all stages of life—children, teen-agers, young adults, parents, married couples and older persons.

"They come from all walks of life—Army officers, stock-

[1] Irma Sampson, "Pastoral Counselling Center Serves People in All Walks of Life," The First Community Church News, Vol. 12, No. 30, Sept. 18–24, 1966, p. 2.

brokers, clerks, social workers, doctors, restaurant managers, dentists, secretaries, teachers, mechanics and housewives . . ."[2]

The scope of services offered in such a clinic depends on the available funds, the size of the church, the nature of the ministry. In New York City, a great clinic such as that run by the American Foundation of Religion and Psychiatry, founded by the Rev. Dr. Norman Vincent Peale and the late Dr. Smiley Blanton, offers services that range from group therapy and psychoanalytic counseling to a "job changing" clinic, marriage counseling, child guidance, and social programs—all staffed by the finest professionals obtainable. But even the smaller churches may have a consulting psychiatrist.

Development of the pastoral counseling program in the United States and abroad stems from the interrelationship of the pastor, the psychiatrist, and the psychological, emotional, and spiritual needs of the congregation. The true sophistication of the modern clergy is apparent on this new frontier. Surveys made by the Academy of Religion and Mental Health indicate that most parishioners in need of guidance for themselves or someone close to them turn first to the priest or minister. "What can I do? Where can I turn?" are the questions the pastor hears again and again, as individuals sit before him, frightened, concerned, unsure, convinced that their case is different from any other the minister has heard.

More than ten percent of all the psychiatrists in the United States are members of the Academy. The total group also includes more than 3,000 pastors, psychologists, psychoanalysts, behavioral scientists, social workers, and mental health workers. Here, workers in the field of psychological need and those in spiritual guidance are joined in an approach that involves the church at both the human and professional levels.

By 1965, these issues had become so important that the Na-

---

[2] *Ibid.*, p. 2.

tional Council of Churches called for a program to explore the possibilities of an academy of parish clergy that would help ministers keep informed of the latest approaches of psychology in dealing with pastoral problems.

"The day is over," declared the Council in a statement to the press, "when a pastor can rely primarily on the seminary training he received a decade or two ago to carry out his parish ministry . . ."

Dr. Karl Menninger, one of the great psychiatric authorities of modern times, accepted the pastor's role as valid—and often essential—in psychiatric therapy. He felt that public worship and shared ritual, the singing together of hymns, the common relationship of the group to the leader-pastor, could all be valuable psychologically as well as religiously in the stimulation of the group relationship, the furtherance of interpersonal relationships, and the turning of the individual from often destructive self-preoccupation.

"Going to church is not equivalent to religion—perhaps not even essential," he declared. "But it is a form of religious activity which comforts, encourages, and supports those for whom its forms and fellowships are acceptable. In this sense it appeals to many psychiatrists as a prescription for patients if not for themselves."[3]

On matters of sin and guilt, Menninger distinguishes between guilt as such and a sense of guilt—guilt that relates to an actual offense and the sense of guilt that relates to imaginary offenses. Patients who consult psychiatrists often feel extreme guilt for some deed they have not committed.

"If such individuals were to go to a judge and ask to be sentenced for this sin, the judge would be astonished; if they were to go to a priest, he would no doubt assure them that they had never done anything and therefore had no guiltiness and there-

---

[3] Karl Menninger, M.D. *Religio-Psychiatric, Religion and Human Behaviour.* Edited by Simon Doniger, Ph.D. New York: Association Press, 1954, p. 3.

fore *should* not have any *sense* of guilt even when they have no actual guilt. There is nothing the priest can do about it except to send them to a psychiatrist! For, on the other hand, there *is* something a psychiatrist can do about it. A psychiatrist can, with scientific tools now at his disposal, ascertain the unconscious, invisible reasons for the false sense of guilt attached to a non-existent sinful or criminal act."[4]

Menninger's statement defines the area in this field of real guilt versus false, the sick guilt of the mind. It highlights the role of the modern church in seeking to understand, to grasp basic psychological and psychiatric ideas that differentiate between the sick and the well.

The church of our times has been shaped by the needs and demands of a bewildered humanity. It has been shaped by men such as Paul Tillich, Dietrich Bonhoeffer, Martin Buber, and Roger Shinn, men of religion who have dared to say new things about old truths, to make these truths more purposeful to the present age, to lift a tangled world, as Shinn calls it, out of senseless patterns of self-destruction.

Churches all over America today offer counseling services because of these needs; the minister of the modern American church is the repository of the social, personal, spiritual, emotional, financial, and even professional problems of his congregation.

In virtually all seminaries, psychiatry is studied from both the clinical and the layman's point of view. Many clergymen spend as much as half their time in counseling, according to the Academy of Religion and Mental Health.

While it appears true that the Protestant churches, particularly the Episcopalian, the United Churches of Christ, and the Lutheran, have been trailblazers in the establishment of such clinics, all religions today are active in the field in varying measure.

---

[4] *Ibid.,* p. 7.

The Catholic Church in the United States, while clinging firmly to fundamental articles of faith (including the reality of personal demons), nevertheless has found room for the purely materialistic psychiatric approach and has achieved many break-throughs in relating religion and psychiatry more closely.

Hundreds of Roman Catholic priests today are trained psy-chiatrists and psychologists. Hundreds of conferences and semi-nars on psychic problems in religious counseling are held in Catholic seminaries; the students in these seminaries are well aware of every new development in these fields. At St. John's University, Collegeville, Minnesota, a mental health institute has been established whose seminars, meetings, dialogues, and work-shops are designed to teach practical techniques of pastoral counseling and psychotherapeutic aid. Clergymen of all faiths have attended these sessions. In Catholic hospitals and youth-guidance centers, psychiatric care is now provided and is in-creasing.

These new attitudes and psychological approaches have greatly shifted the emphasis of religion. Side by side with the road to the confessional one finds an additional trail to the com-passion of psychological counseling, guidance and professional treatment as needed.

A brochure published by the National Association for Mental Health and prepared by the Rev. Thomas W. Klink, Methodist minister associated with the Menninger School of Psychiatry, and Supervising Chaplain of the Topeka State Hospital in Kansas, includes a prayer written by a patient at that hospital shortly after she emerged from deep emotional disturbance:

"O Eternal God, whose mercy is never failing, and whose steady sureness is ever around us, we have not always trusted Thee. Forgive us, when we have trusted the testimony of our fears, when we have questioned the unchanging reality of Thy creation. Thou knowest that we have sometimes felt as though our thoughts had distorted Thy goodness. Forgive us all our sins and all the deeds of our illness. We are together again, and we confess Thee as sure and merciful, a solid rock of our confidence. Set our feet on the steady earth, we pray, and let our hearts find rest in Thee. . . ."[5]

It is a cry of release—and of hunger for God. For religion, by accepting psychiatry, does not forfeit a part of its relationship with Deity. Rather it opens an avenue to expanding understanding and new dimensions.

Nowhere is this more apparent than in modern man's need to deal with his own guilt—real or imagined—and to find his way to forgiveness.

---

[5] The Rev. Thomas W. Klink. *Clergymen's Guide to Recognizing Serious Mental Illness*. New York: The National Association for Mental Health, Inc.

SIN, GUILT, AND GOD

What constitutes sin is a question that has haunted religion across the years, but the answer has never been so completely confused as in the modern church. New approaches to sin, some of which we have already explored, not only leave many laymen puzzled; even more important, they leave the church itself unsure.

Basically sin has always been separation from God, wholly or in part, permanently or temporarily, as the result of an individual's acts of commission or omission. Sin itself has been pinpointed and precise, especially in Roman Catholicism, where the penance was equally specific. The new theologies, however, have added many modifications of the definition of sin, most of which involve the causes of the allegedly sinful act. These, in turn, leave a wide field for ambivalence and contradictions. Murder, says society, is evil and sinful in the eyes of the church. But abortion, which many religious people call a kind of murder, is not considered sinful in large areas of the new church.

And even the most vicious and cold-blooded murder, not of the unborn but of the born, also may be excused in instances where social and environmental causes are regarded as primarily responsible. So also with rape, robbery, mugging, and other violence. "Who is really guilty?" asks the new church in many cases. "The criminal? Or we who do nothing to change the conditions that produced this alleged murderer?"

There is no easy answer in Christian terms as understood by new religious morality. This has nothing to do with the law or legal action. The question becomes: Is the youth guilty in terms of actually separating himself from God by this act? Or is God's instant forgiveness already available?

Again, in the confusions of religious upheaval, personal commitment to a belief in God and salvation through Jesus Christ appears no longer enough to gain acceptance in heaven. In the minds of many pastors, the social commitment—dedication to social needs, to the removal of community injustices and inequities, to active sidewalk participation in societal debate—becomes essential to the personal commitments that lead to eternal salvation. This becomes the new road, the good news of the gospels redefined, reinterpreted.

It is a wide change from the early evangelism. The alcoholic walking the sawdust trail discovers that it is not enough to commit himself to God and leave it at that. There must also be added commitment to desegregation, to just laws and wages, to proper working conditions, to a host of activities to which worldly involvement is an additional requirement for eternal salvation. It is a new kind of involvement, on a mass basis, a commitment to the modern mass-population world.

The Social Creed of the Methodist Church, adopted in 1964, declares:

"The Methodist Church must view the perplexing times and problems which we face in the light of the life and teachings of Jesus. Jesus taught us to love our neighbours, and seek justice for them as well as for ourselves. To be silent in the face of need, injustice, and exploitation is to deny Him.

"We believe that God is Father of all people and races, that

Jesus Christ is His Son, that all men are brothers, and that each person is of infinite worth as a child of God.

"We believe that 'the earth is the Lord's and the fullness thereof.' Our own capacities and all we possess are gifts of the Creator, and should be held and used in stewardship to Him.

"We believe that God is Christ in seeking to redeem all men and also society. This redemption is a continuing necessity.

"We believe that the grace of God in Christ is available for redemption from individual and social sin as we seek in penitence and obedience to do His holy will . . ."

The program outlined in this document delineates in detail the church's position, largely traditional and unarguable, on many problems of individuals and groups, ranging from opposition to gambling, promiscuity in sex, pornography, and sale of drugs on the illicit market, to the need for developing new programs for mental health, medical care, human rights, world peace, proper working conditions for labor; for finding solutions for alcoholic problems; for abstention from the use of alcohol; for application or redemptive principles in dealing with law offenders; and for the right to exemption from military service for all within the Methodist Church who cannot in good conscience perform such service.

The Methodists' views are echoed in other Protestant faiths. Many fundamentalist and evangelical churches put increasing emphasis on service to the world, even while clinging to their pitchfork metaphysics. The fire-and-brimstone pastors have softened their position a little in favor of a new emphasis on worldly needs.

Part of the church's difficulty in dealing with modern sin and guilt revolves around the question of emphasis. The new church is not only locked in controversy on individual versus social salvation; it is also concerned with the techniques of repentance and the obtaining of God's forgiveness.

New concepts of God's forgiveness seem to be taking shape.

The church for years has built its role in these matters on the formalistic and ritualistic; we kneel and pray, we routinely murmur the words and phrases, the familiar repetitions, the *mea culpa*s, we tell ourselves we are really sorry about all this killing overseas or whatever the particular issue or sin may be, we sip the wine and taste the wafer and hear the sacred words—and our sin and guilt are gone.

No more. In the relative morality, sin is not an absolute; we deal in evaluation and interpretation; it becomes more and more difficult, almost impossible in many instances, to commit absolute sin by today's lights.

Sin, repent, and God forgives. In some cases this translates into: Whatever you have done, it has cause; the cause rather than you must be forgiven and possibly removed.

The fact of the contraceptive pill is a causal force of change in modern morality, and therefore in the church and its teachings.

Chaplains and pastors associated with American colleges are constantly facing young couples who cannot or will not marry but who do not consider premarital or nonmarital sexual relations sinful. The pill virtually eliminates the peril of unpleasant results; it is easily available, it cannot be controlled; children can obtain it almost as easily as adults. And even the Roman Catholic priest or Protestant minister often reinforces the words of the family doctor: "If she is going to have premarital sexual relations, is it not better that she at least avoid the added sin of bearing a child no one wants?"

Even more controversial has been the attitude of church groups, led particularly by the Episcopalians, on the question of abortion. Once a taboo subject, abortion has become both a political and religious battleground. Too many women with unwelcome pregnancies have been impelled to have illegal operations; it is estimated that 100,000 or more die each year from abortions.

The Roman Catholic position has been sharply questioned but

—at least as late as 1968—it has remained unchanged. Catholicism sees the prevention of procreation by artificial means as a basic sin against Divine Law. Even stronger is its attitude against abortion; if anyone must die, the church says, it must be the mother; the passive, helpless infant must be protected.

But if most Catholic prelates hold firm to what they consider immutable absolutes, the same is not true of members of their flock. Pressures among Catholics to effect changes within the church have risen to fever pitch. Large numbers of Catholic wives admit that they use the birth-control pill or other artificial means to prevent conception and state that if they cannot gain absolution by confessing their sin they simply fail to mention it. Many who do try to follow the decrees on birth control are urging the church openly to adopt a more realistic approach. *Newsweek* magazine, in a survey in the spring of 1967, found that one in every three Catholic wives uses contraceptive pills and seventy percent of all Catholics favor repeal of the contraception ban.

But neither the church nor its priesthood discount the efficacy of confession, whatever the status of the sin or the sinner. Confession in the sacred confines of the confessional, through the priest as intermediary, presents a release of tremendous psychological importance apart from its religious character. Whether or not one has faith in the forgiveness of God, the burden of guilt or imagined guilt is lifted by this means.

Considered psychologically, the act of confession has a completeness about it in relationship to the mind, a purging of guilt by confession, by the statement itself. *I did it, I confess, I admit, I am sorry, grievously sorry and the burden of guilt is heavy upon me, too heavy, intolerable.*

For those who open their beings to the ritual of forgiving love, the psychologists themselves admit, confession to God can become a ritual that truly heals.

Apart from the formal theological and confessional aspects of sin, its shape and definition in actual practice have changed in Roman Catholicism—and far more radically so in other churches.

Starkly different from the Catholic—yet surprisingly parallel in some aspects—are the far more modern concepts of the United Church of Christ, which comprises a number of denominations that came together formally in 1957. The church has more than two million members and nearly seven thousand congregations. Denominations that participated in its unions and mergings over a century of worship have included the Congregational Methodist Church, the Congregational Churches, the Evangelical Protestants, the Christian Church, and the Evangelical Synod of North America and the Reformed Church in the United States. The last two had joined in 1934 under the name Evangelical and Reformed Church.

A statement of faith issued by the United Church of Christ in January, 1965, declares:

"Most members believe that God's Word is spoken in the Scriptures, but do not equate the Scriptures with the Word of God, as if everything in them were His own truth. It is generally accepted that while God's Word is to be found primarily in the Bible, the Scriptures are not necessarily the last word—that there is still more light and truth to break forth from God's Holy Word."

On the question of church teaching about sin and salvation, which might well be stated as "guilt and forgiveness," the United Church statement declares that God seeks "in holy love to save all people from aimlessness and sin."

"Men sin—in fear, in hostility, pride, greed, unconcern. The God we know in Christ forgives those who trust him and draws his people into the love that overcomes sin."

Later the statement says: "There is firm belief that God is the final judge of men and that He offers men eternal life. Beyond that belief is much that we do not know. Many United Church leaders think it is better to trust in God than to theorize about details they cannot know."

Millions in the more conservative Protestant churches, as well as millions in the Roman Catholic faith, cannot accept so liberal or so vague an interpretation of God's role in this world—or the next. But there is also evidence that, while many churches hold firmly to the established creeds and dogmas, individual members hold widely varying opinions as to just how far they go intellectually in accepting the spelled-out details of God's role in our lives, or of how God's forgiveness is or is not obtained.

In this regard a survey was undertaken by Yoshio Fukuyama of the United Church Board of Homeland Ministries in association with Dr. Thomas Campbell of the Divinity School of Yale University. Entitled *The Parishioners, A Sociological Interpretation,* this survey polled more than 8,500 members of the United Church concerning their ideas on religious questions. Although all questioned were currently members of the United Church, they came from varied religious backgrounds, including Lutheran, Presbyterian, Episcopal, and Roman Catholic homes and upbringing. Since the questionnaires were unidentifiable, respondents could answer freely. On the questions regarding sin, guilt, and hell, the answers were extraordinarily revealing. Although more than three-fourths affirmed belief that Jesus rose from the dead, and an even greater number affirmed their faith that God revealed Himself to man in Jesus Christ, less than half affirmed that sin is separation from God, only slightly more than a quarter believed that all men are born guilty of original sin, and less than twenty percent believed that Hell is a just punishment for sinners.

Man's free will to choose between right and wrong, regardless of other factors, remains at the core of most of the Christian belief. And this becomes an issue of conscience. We choose—but do we choose aright? An official of the National Council of Churches once told this writer: "The little Southern lady who goes to church regularly and is kind to everyone and loves God and Jesus, but who doesn't believe that white and Negro should sit side by side, even in church, is guilty of an un-Christian act."

Thus the sin that today appears to outpace all others, according to the official at the National Council, is not the violation of church law in the eyes of many modern authorities; it is the sin of not caring for others, knowingly not caring, aware of the hurt but remaining untouched, disinterested, unmoved to action.

The iconoclastic Episcopal priest, the Rev. Malcolm Boyd, believes that only by leaving the well-trodden paths of conformity, by shunning the accepted, ritualistic, safe and sane roads where all questions have already been asked and answered, does Christianity itself become alive.

"Christianity," he notes, "is revolutionary, radical, shaking, relating every part of human life to every other part of human life. It is not some cult of religiosity which hands out spiritual tranquilizers and builds a doll-house church life. It is not a fantasy. Christianity is based on the reality of God's redeeming love for man. This is love that recognizes that it must extend to social justice. One cannot claim to love God if he does not love his brother. Christianity involves a Christian in politics, race relations, religion, economics, sociology . . . in every aspect of human life."[1]

During the racial riots in Detroit in 1967 a television news reporter stopped a Negro and asked him, "What do you want?" And the Negro answered, "Nothing." Then later he added, "You wouldn't understand."

The Rev. Michael Nesbitt of St. Michael's in the Fields Episcopal Church in Toledo, Ohio, related this incident to his congregation. Discussing the Negro's remark the pastor asked his listeners, "Is it too much to realize that what he meant was, 'I don't want anything you can give me—by your action-success

[1] Malcolm Boyd, *Youth and Christ*. Cincinnati, Ohio: Forward Movement Publications, 1964.

ability—by your technological know-how, by your ability to take my problems away, solve them through a computer and hand them back in a neat package all processed and wrapped in cellophane so they're not ever mine anymore'?

"Is it too much to realize that he meant, 'I desire to be human—to have a definitive say in the decisions that program my life and that of my family'? Is it too much in the Church for us to realize that what he meant was, 'I am a child of God—but you who go to church don't seem to know it'?"

It is clear in all of these new attitudes that sin is different, is no longer the absolute, but is relative to the needs of the world. Sin has new dimensions because it involves new thinking, new responsibilities to God's word, the church of our time is clearly stating. Are we for abortion—or for ruinous overpopulation and agonizing mass starvation of millions, as already is happening in India?

The new dimension of sin, the church insists, reaches out to the world, and the sin lies, in any of a thousand forms, in failing to meet this modern responsibility. The guilt cannot be absolved by a half dozen Our Father's in some quiet pew; the new expiation of the sin lies not in ritual but in concern and action for the world.

It is in the deed, rather than the word, says the new church. It is in the prayer, not for absolution but for vision and purpose, that we may begin to absolve ourselves.

CHAPTER V

———◆●◆———

AND WHEN YOU PRAY

Religious change in our times concerns not only the tangible and visible church but even more importantly the lines of communication between man and God. This, in turn, concerns prayer.

There are new kinds of prayer and new words to meet the meanings and yearnings of our age. At the same time true prayer must remain a sacred road that has no part of the profane, of incantations or drugged hallucinations.

This is the searching test that is faced by modern prayer in a world where victims of LSD or marijuana sometimes pray in church without knowing even where they are, or sometimes kneel in worship before trees or pray to far-off clouds.

To a barefoot man in a musty former movie house on New York's Second Avenue, the shadowed auditorium before him was church, and the bearded youths and frowsy-haired girls were his prayerful flock. His name was Dr. Timothy Leary, former Harvard faculty member, who was preaching in that winter of 1967 a doctrine of the greatness of a new drug called LSD. "Prayer is not words alone; it's an attitude," he told his listeners.

"Think of it as a thin red thread extending from the world within you into the world outside your body. Then you will never have a bad trip"—by which he meant a bad experience with the dangerous drug—"and will never become psychotic."

Earlier in this extraordinary "religious service" conducted by Dr. Leary and his League for Spiritual Discovery, the bearded Greenwich Village poet Allen Ginsburg sat crossed-legged in the lotus position; while an associate strummed some kind of Asiatic instrument, Ginsburg rhythmically struck a brass triangle and chanted in Sanskrit to "the Buddha Yet to Manifest": "Om Shri Maitre Ya." The same four words, to Buddha, intoned over and over again with hypnotic repetition.

This ancient form of prayer recalled other chantings, other prayers repeated over and over in ritualistic form in fully accepted religions within the Christian-Judaic churches and in other great religions of the world.

The chanted mantra to LSD performed by a poet who believes everybody should smoke "pot" seemed to this writer one of the more bizarre aspects of our current ferment and sometimes frenzy—even in prayer.

Prayer in churches today has taken two basic directions. One is the reaching out to theatrical effects, to allegedly "oriental" teachings, such as West Coast prayer wheels patterned after those found in parts of Tibet and Outer Mongolia, and the use of drugs to aid in the achievement of trance-communion with God. An outstanding example is found in the writings of the late Aldous Huxley about his "religio-narcotic" experiences with sense-distorting drugs such as mescaline and peyotl.

The second direction of prayer is rather to the reality and need of the world, a form of prayer that is both acceptance and understanding, that invokes no Buddha or anything of the kind. Yet it does raise basic questions as to what kind of prayer is acceptable to Deity. Are the formal incantations necessary, in our own or any other language, to the achievement of the intimate communion between Him and ourselves?

Reading one of the most magnificent examples of prayer cited by Jesus—the tax collector's brief, "Lord, be merciful to me, a sinner"—one cannot help wondering if proper prayer requires all the decorative salutations, if indeed God desires any such approach, or needs our reminder that He is both mighty and merciful. Are the flowery phrases and the Old English "Thees and Thous" likely to make the prayer more honest—or less?

Consider an example of the new approach in a prayer by Malcolm Boyd, who clings to the traditional in basic theology yet omits entirely the familiar threadbare phraseology. Without mantras and chanting that become almost pagan, the content of his prayer is as close as our next-door neighbor. Consider a prayer from the book *Are You Running With Me, Jesus?*:

"God:

"Take fire and burn away our guilt and our lying hypocrisies.

"Take water and wash away our brothers' blood which we have caused to shed.

"Take hot sunlight and dry the tears of those we have hurt, and heal their wounded souls, minds, and bodies.

"Take love and root it in our hearts, so that brotherhood may grow, transforming the dry desert of our prejudices and hatreds.

"Take our imperfect prayers and purify them, so that we mean what we pray and are prepared to give ourselves to you along with our words, through Jesus Christ, who did not disdain to take humanness upon him and live among us, sharing our life, our joys, and our pains.

"Amen."[1]

Thus Father Boyd, whose prayers are often shaking but never profane.

"Only a relatively small group in the church today," Father Boyd told me, "is striving to make it more relevant, striving to bring Christian love into segments where there is usually only scorn. Racial separation, discrimination, and racist persecution

---

[1] Malcolm Boyd, *Are You Running With Me, Jesus?* New York, Chicago, San Francisco: Holt, Rinehart and Winston, 1965, p. 119.

remain the primary examples of this. Poverty and urban decay continue relentlessly in our nominally Christian society. Peace is elusive in our military-oriented economy. Antisemitism lurks always just beneath the surface of public professions of Christian love. I know a church in California (to turn to yet another example) where two homosexuals—two persons who deeply needed Christian compassion and understanding—were publicly asked not to come to worship in that church.

"In my book, *Are You Running With Me, Jesus?*, I have a prayer regarding homosexuals which many people think to be extremely moving, yet a number of churches at which I have spoken recently to young groups have asked me specifically not to read that prayer."

Because of his new ideas regarding prayer and other forms of worship and reverence, concepts by which knowingly or unknowingly he implements Bonhoeffer's idea of "holy worldliness," Boyd often finds himself in sharp disagreement with the traditionalist approaches. Of one encounter he stated:

"A fundamentalist recently told me that all Jews, Moslems, Buddhists, agnostics, atheists were going to a literal hell where hell-fire would be the worst torture imaginable and would continue eternally. He said that Eichmann, because he reputedly confessed his sins before he died, is now in heaven, but the six million Jews for whose murders he was at least in large part responsible are suffering the tortures of the damned in hell. There is no salvation for those in hell, the fundamentalist said, and he reiterated that only 'saved-again Christians' have access to the place he calls heaven."

What a travesty of Divine love it would be—six million souls condemned to eternal agony because they did not join the right church! Even the children Christ likened to the Kingdom of Heaven itself!

A parallel to the approach of Father Boyd is found in the prayers of the modern French Roman Catholic priest Abbé

Michel Quoist. Abbé Quoist is a priest of the working people, the priest of the problems of the nameless toilers of fields, factories, docks, and sea; of their wives and children; of their frustrations, their bitterness, their joy, their guilt, their fear.

His book *Prayers* has been read by millions in France and throughout Europe and in translations in England and America.

Abbé Quoist loves people. He finds them and reaches out to them in his prayers with his own love, which serves also as a channel of God's love. But again, as with Father Boyd, this love is expressed not in the traditional phraseology, or the mouthings of alleged adoration, but in the simplicities of the prosaic, the mundane. In words that tingle with immediacy he writes in the closing lines of a prayer he calls "The Telephone":

"Since I didn't listen, I learned nothing.

Since I didn't listen, I didn't help.

Since I didn't listen, we didn't commune.

Forgive me, Lord, for we were connected,

And now we are cut off."[2]

The reform movement within the Roman Catholic Church has helped immensely in opening doors to modernity. The fact that the language of the people of our times—and our own lands—is now used in the Mass and in other services, rituals, and prayers has revealed whole new meanings and spiritual realities within the Catholic circle, and it has encouraged leaders of other faiths to break from tradition wherever it is clung to solely for tradition's sake.

Catholicism has long held a basic and almost unassailable position in regard to the essence of prayer. Prayer, according to the Catholic Church, can be defined most simply as "the lifting up of our minds and hearts to God." This, it seems to me, asserts clearly two things: first, that prayer is a relationship of the individual to God and His universe, and second, that the whole being

---

[2] Michel Quoist, *Prayers*. Translated by Agnes M. Forsyth and Anne Marie deCommaille. New York: Sheed and Ward Inc., 1963, p. 19.

of the individual must reach out in this experience to God, the Source.

Here, the Catholic Church reveals its own unchanging concept most clearly; neither traditional nor modern words alter the core of meaning.

But while the tradition exists and will continue as a part of worship and ritual, new currents are found here as in other aspects of worship. The prayer of affirmation becomes more important than the prayer of petition; we are no longer so sure that we are correct in trying to bribe God with our words of praise, to force our will upon Divinity.

Writers such as Teilhard de Chardin, the "cosmic Catholic" who has defined modern Christian thought in terms at once worldly and divine, bring to Catholicism new substance with which to endow old prayers, new interpretations of old petitions.

In *The Phenomena of Man,* Chardin asserts that man is capable of discovering his God in the whole length, breadth, and depth of a world in movement. "To be able literally to say to God that one loves Him, not only with all one's body, all one's heart, and all one's soul, but with every fibre of the unifying universe—that is a prayer that only can be made in space time."

The long, involved dialectic prayers in which the man in the pulpit outlines a whole five-year program for God's action is still a part of the phenomena of Sunday. Yet there is at the same time a rebellion against the phenomena, sometimes outspoken, sometimes merely indicated by nonparticipation in the lengthy detailed petition, often more properly called demands.

In the thinking of moderns such as Teilhard de Chardin, Father Boyd, Abbé Quoist, and others, such leading prayers are almost an insult to Deity. They ask for special favors, for advantages. They tell God that we are wiser than He; we know who should win the election, the ball game, the prize fight, the war. It is because too many pray or have prayed in this fashion that the prayer of petition has fallen into disfavor.

The author recalls debating on a radio program with the Reverend Robert Schrock, pastor of Sts. Paul and Peter Methodist Church in New York.

"Why should we ask God for special favors for ourselves?" Schrock challenged. "Are we not in that case exactly like a superstitious tribesman praying to the God of thunder and lightning not to strike his thatched hut, or the soldier on the front lines, praying for the bullet to hit somebody else, not him?"

But, I rejoined, did he not consider the Lord's prayer to be a petition when it asks: "Give us this day, our daily bread, and forgive us our debts as we forgive our debtors"?

He agreed that it was; but not, he pointed out, a petition for a private miracle. "It is only a plea to let us be a proper part of universal laws and functionings. It doesn't ask God to turn those laws upside down as a special favor we think we need."

It is a fact that many who leave formal religion do so because their prayers seem unavailing. It is equally true that many of the young people of today, and the young clergymen, have become increasingly interested in Eastern cults and religions, particularly Zen, because of the emphasis placed on affirmation, the prayer that does not ask, but seeks only to accept. It is at once an acceptance of God's will and an awareness that God's will for us is love, cosmic and all-powerful, love that can be ours unless it is in some way blocked out. Our affirmation, our acceptance, our surrender becomes, in its ultimate form, our prayer.

Another allied development on the way-out fringes of faith in the United States concerns the increasing role of Indian yogis and gurus. A combination of revived interest in Oriental thinking and belief coupled with the quest of the young for new avenues of religious outlets has helped to popularize the meditation movement.

The phenomenal British music, the Beatles, has helped to develop the movement by their interest in a particular guru known as the Maharishi (full name Maharishi Mahesh Yogi), whose teachings follow a transcendental line. The Maharishi has visited Europe and America to spread his belief that suffering is unnecessary and to teach others how to develop "God-consciousness" within themselves. He calls this his "spiritual regeneration movement."

The Maharishi has long graying hair, a graying beard, and a sizable black moustache. He speaks the simple language of metaphysics with a heavy accent on the role of peace and meditation and with a deep faith in the Oriental belief in reincarnation. The meditation movement has both its good and bad aspects. It is a symptom of search. It also opens the door for a developing and fragmenting cultism that could weaken the role of soundly based modern religious activity and exploration.

What is probably closest to truth today is that no single way of prayer, type of prayer, can be wholly right or wrong, nor can any single place be the one place for prayer. The little girl bowing with her petition before the statue of St. Mary is as right in her way as the intellectual of faith who sits alone in the pew of the empty church, communing in the silence with Deity, surrendering his being to his affirmation of God.

At the same time, new thinking, ideas, and words *are* helping to make our prayers more relevant. There is a balance that keeps us on track, that does not go to extremes of drugs and incantations, despite some current experimentation by individuals within the church and the clergy. The fad of the religious extremes begins to recede.

No one has probed these metaphysical areas with all their complex difficulties more deeply and revealingly than Martin Buber, one of the greatest influences on religious thinking and religious renewal in this country. In *I and Thou,* Buber speaks of man as needing God and God as needing man. He speaks of prayer and sacrifice as two great servants who "pace through the ages."

"What distinguishes sacrifice and prayer from all magic?" he asks in *I and Thou*. "Magic desires to obtain its effects without entering into relation, and practices its tricks in the void. But sacrifice and prayer are set 'before the Face,' in the consummation of the holy primary word that means mutual action: they speak the *Thou,* and then they hear."[3]

Thus, to Buber, prayer is relationship, pure relationship; and it cannot be pure dependence on one side only, he insists, for this empties the relationship of reality. Each depends upon the other, it is an interrelationship of Being and action, of I and Thou, and knowing this becomes the prayer, the sacrifice, the answer, the victory.

Nevertheless, Buber's intellectualism to the contrary notwithstanding, other elements of modern prayer and worship—in and out of church—turn to areas that come frighteningly close to magic and incantation.

---

[3] Martin Buber, *I and Thou*. New York: Charles Scribner's Sons, 1958, p. 83.

WHO SPEAK IN TONGUES

Glossolalia, otherwise called speaking in tongues, is one new direction of concern and alarm.

In 1960, Father Dennis Bennett, the much-admired and re-spected rector of St. Mark's Episcopal Church in Van Nuys, California, announced from the pulpit that he had been meeting with persons who "spoke in strange tongues," that he himself had spoken in words he did not understand, and that he felt this was an area of religious importance in which others of the congrega-tion might want to participate.

The reaction was immediate and explosive. Some worshipers in the two-thousand-member parish were outraged. One priest refused to continue at the service. Vestrymen demanded that Father Bennett resign at once. Stories of the "outbreak" of glossolalia were carried in newspapers throughout the country. Father Bennett was replaced, and the Bishop of Los Angeles, the Rt. Rev. Francis Eric Bloy, sent out a pastoral letter summarily banning any further speaking in tongues under the auspices of the church. There were assertions, however, that hundreds within the church personally wanted to investigate the subject of speaking in tongues.

The speakers in strange tongues have found a place for themselves in some of the most conservative churches in the country. Not everyone in such churches accepts services in which prominent members kneel to pray in gibberish. But many have welcomed this development, and growing numbers are investigating the revived "gift" of the spirit, its validity or lack of it, its meaning in the modern church.

California newspapers cited rumors of a revival of speaking in tongues in other parts of the country: in Southern states, and particularly in the Pentecostal churches. Methodist Bishop Gerald Kennedy of California rejected claims that speaking in tongues could be of spiritual benefit to the church and its people.

Father Bennett explained that he had discussed the subject with others, that he himself had experienced Baptism of the Holy Spirit and that along with it had come the "gift of tongues." This is glossolalia—an experience in which the individual speaks in language, phrases, and words he himself does not understand. Sometimes he speaks in "strange tongues," languages of other lands and peoples; and sometimes in "unknown tongues," words that seem to have no meaning, sounds of gibberish. In churches that accept this form of "gift" theologically, some members are said to have the gift of hearing these languages inwardly—or of interpreting the words of others who speak in tongues.

Still others, however, prefer to accept the definition of Harper's *Bible Dictionary*, which defines glossolalia as "inarticulate and unintelligible speech, meaningless sounds, jargon, uttered in times of extreme emotional excitement or religious frenzy." Regarding this gift and meaning there is, certainly, wide divergence of both theological and lay opinion.

Father Bennett was shifted to a small church in Seattle, Washington, where it was expected that he would cease his efforts in the field of glossolalia, but reports indicate the contrary. Under his pastorship, Baptism of the Holy Spirit and speaking in tongues has become a new force in the community among both the clergy and the congregation.

What is speaking in tongues, physically, spiritually? Is it more than hysterical gibberish? Can it possibly have spiritual force of any sort? One would be tempted to give an instant negative to these questions were it not for the large number of persons claiming to have had the Baptism of the Holy Spirit and the gift of tongues, and were it not true that glossolalia is being practiced or at least investigated in many organized religions. This pertains not merely to the Pentecostal and Evangelical churches, but to many other congregations—including Lutherans, Episcopalians, and Methodists—normally not associated with extreme forms of worship.

The theological basis on which the gift of tongues has gained some acceptance rests on the Bible, the most important citation being that regarding Pentecost in the Book of Acts. At that time, fifty days after the Crucifixion and Resurrection, many Christians, it is recorded, including Mary, the mother of Jesus, and his "brothers," came together in "an upper room" in ancient Jerusalem. Present also were all of the disciples of Jesus except Judas.

A number of remarkable events occurring on that Pentecostal day are described in one of the most vivid pieces of writing in the Book of Acts:

"And when the Day of Pentecost was fully come, they were all with one accord in one place. . . . And they were all filled with the Holy Ghost, and began to speak with other tongues, as the Spirit gave them utterance.

"And there were dwelling at Jerusalem Jews, devout men, out of every nation under heaven. Now when this was noised abroad, the multitude came together, and were confounded, because that every man heard them speak in his own language . . .

"And they were all amazed and marvelled. . . ."[1]

From this passage many take differing meanings, including the Seventh Day Adventists, who point out that the people present presumably *heard* in differing tongues words spoken by the same individual. The Adventists' interpretation, however, does not consider the fact that the same passage refers to those present as *speaking* in differing tongues. This is an indication of how diversely the passage can be and has been interpreted over the centuries.

Additional Biblical references are found in the letters of St. Paul. Asserting that it is wrong to prevent those who would speak in tongues from doing so, Paul also indicates that to him the gift of prophecy is far more important. In his first letter to the Corinthians, Paul lists gifts of the Spirit, among which he includes speaking in tongues and also interpretation of tongues.

While Biblical acceptance of the gift is thus given by Paul, he also warns strenuously against misusing it.

From Paul's writing it is clear that the Corinthians, steeped in the religious traditions of ancient Greece, reverted to wild, earthy language, even the women breaking out into brazen vulgarities. Paul warned that speaking in tongues was permissible in public worship, but only under specific controls: Only one person should speak at a time. Women should remain silent, because "it is unseemly for a woman to speak in church." In the tones of a loving but concerned prelate, he tells them, in closing his epistle to the church of Corinth, "Let all things be done properly and in order."

Only a few other reports of glossolalia are found in early Christian records, and even these have been questioned by scholars. Origen, a church writer of the first half of the third century, reports vaguely that some religious persons of his century spoke in tongues; but the details are too indefinite for exact

---

[1] The Acts II: 1, 4–7.

examination even as to the identities of the speakers. During the Middle Ages and the Reformation, instances of glossolalia are found on both the Roman Catholic and the Protestant sides. Certain extreme members of the Jansenist Movement in eighteenth-century France were said to speak in tongues; the Jansenists eventually denounced the practice.

In nineteenth-century England, a group of speakers in tongues founded what became known as the Catholic Apostolic Church. The movement was also called Irvingism, after its founder, Edward Irving. The near hysteria of its members brought them widespread criticism. The Presbyterian Church, to which Irving originally belonged, hurriedly disavowed any connection with him. The small following of the Catholic Apostolic Church of modern times claims no connection with Irvingism, or with the earlier church's unusual forms of worship.

In America movements of varied sorts flared up in the colonies and the early United States, but these sporadic developments did not take definitive form until the major rebirth of glossolalia at the beginning of the twentieth century. At that time a Methodist minister named Charles F. Parkham, seeking new ways to achieve the Baptism of the Holy Spirit, broke with his church and gathered followers and students who sought the Baptism and the gifts of the Holy Spirit. In a rented house in Topeka, Kansas—an unfinished mansion known as Stone's Folly, after the man who started to build the over-ambitious edifice—Parkham and his students prayed regularly, practiced the laying on of hands, and constantly sought to receive the Holy Spirit and its evidential gift of tongues.

One day a young woman student asked Parkham to put his hands upon her head as she knelt in prayer. As he did so, words began to pour forth from her lips, words neither she nor Parkham understood.

John L. Sherrill, an editor of the magazine *Guideposts,* who has investigated glossolalia in considerable depth, describes the climactic scene in Stone's Folly in the following vivid passage:

"The Pentecostals look back on this hour—7:00 P.M., New Year's Eve, 1900—as one of the key dates in their history. They point to it as the first time since the days of the early church that the Baptism in the Holy Spirit had been sought, where speaking in tongues was expected as the initial experience.

"At Stone's Folly, everyone now prayed with increased fervor for the coming of the Holy Spirit. One of the large unfinished rooms on the top floor of the mansion was turned into a prayer room in a conscious effort to recreate the setting of the Upper Room in Jerusalem at Pentecost. Over the next three days there were many Baptisms, each one signaled by the mysterious tongues. On January 3, Parkham himself and a dozen other ministers from various denominations present with him in this room received the Baptism, and spoke with tongues."[2]

Out of this beginning was to come the Pentecostal Church, whose growth in the United States and abroad has been an extraordinary story. The belief in the Baptism of the Holy Spirit and the gift of tongues has always been one of the fundamentals of this church.

The spread of speaking in tongues among groups not associated directly or primarily with the Pentecostals began in the 1960's; the West Coast episode, in fact, with its attendant publicity, was one of the first steps in this direction. It reflected two developments in certain sections of American religion: a desire to return to original religious beginnings, and a religious hunger for escape from impersonal ritualism.

Both in America and abroad, the reborn phenomenon of speaking in tongues began to appear. Many group services were held without public announcement because of the possible oppo-

---

[2] John L. Sherrill, *They Speak with Other Tongues*. Westwood, New Jersey, SpireBooks, 1965, p. 38.

sition of some church members. One group calling itself Christian Advance has held meetings throughout America, concentrating on the study and experience of glossolalia in both its speaking and interpretative aspects. Some of these meetings, particularly those held on the West Coast, have attracted huge gatherings, some said to number almost two thousand persons.

One of the leaders of this movement on the East Coast, the Rev. Harold Bredesen, pastor of the First Reformed Church, Mt. Vernon, New York, explained to this writer what he considered the chief reasons behind the gift of tongues:

"I think glossolalia is the means by which, through the prayer and the Baptism of the Holy Spirit, we bypass man's intellectualism, his limited mental abilities to reach out to God. Our minds lack the breadth and scope to comprehend the wonder and glory and meaning of God fully; this is not something that a man can do intellectually. Words fail us and hinder our ability to speak and communicate with Almighty God.

"This is the reason for tongues. It carries us beyond ourselves, our limitations; it lifts us to another level of communication entirely, one in which only the warm glow of human spiritual meaning flows out of us and loses itself in intimate communion with the Being of God."

Following a meeting with Pastor Bredesen, a group of Yale students, including at least one Phi Beta Kappa, began meeting and praying for the "gift," and at least twenty were said to have spoken in tongues. Similar episodes, according to reports in the *Christian Herald* and elsewhere, were said to have happened in universities on the West Coast, including Stanford University and the University of California at Los Angeles.

The sincerity of the participants is hard to doubt. That these people may be over-emotional, or driven by deep inner compulsions of the unconscious mind, also are possibilities that must be considered. At the Lutheran Medical Center in Brooklyn a full-fledged and objective investigation is being conducted. Who and what are these speakers? By what means and for what purpose do they speak thus? Is it for the glory of God or the edification of self? Is it truly a gift of the spirit?

The extent of the revival in the United States in the 1960's was matched by the concern of many of the new intellectuals of the church that this was a diversion from the mainstream of social action and relevance to the modern world.

That there has to be wide divergence of opinion in so controversial a field cannot be doubted. The Right Rev. James A. Pike, Episcopal bishop of California who resigned his see in 1966 because of charges of heresy arising out of his liberal interpretations of the Bible and church doctrine, has described glossolalia as a form of "heresy in embryo." Its more extreme forms he describes as "associated with schizophrenia." The Lutheran Church has members who practice speaking in tongues, but one of this church's leading psychological authorities has described the whole subject as an example of hysteria: "We live in an age of tension and hysteria; this would seem to be one of its forms."

On the other hand Leonard LeSourd, editor of *Guideposts* and one of America's best-informed religious authorities, told me that while he regards speaking in tongues as one of the lesser gifts of the spirit, he and his wife, Catherine Marshall LeSourd, author of *A Man Called Peter,* frequently pray in tongues.

"I don't think this kind of praying should be done in public," he said. "There is always the danger of exhibitionism and even sheer fakery involved and possible. But there are times when I find praying in tongues of great value, particularly when I am puzzled about some problem or what to do about some person in trouble. It is in such moments that I strive to let the words come, the words that may make no sense to me, sounds that may be meaningless and yet seem to be part of something else."

There are dangers, he warned. He cited those who use speaking in tongues as an "emotional kick" rather than a true religious experience. He sounded a warning also against prayer groups that pray in tongues only as a kind of fetish.

"But if there are a few people who pray together in love, in the deep caring and concern for others and their problems—this caring seems to illuminate the whole experience. As I pray I do not necessarily consciously think that now I will pray in tongues, but I let the words take over from me. It is as if I were removed from myself, as if I heard myself speaking without controlling what I said. And sometimes in such moments I feel, I know, that the spirit has taken hold of me, it is there, it is present, it is an exhilarating experience because one receives a sense of calm, of knowing answers that a moment before were not there."

In the variety of modern opinions, attitudes, and approaches to glossolalia, a basic difference is found in what individuals say as individuals and churches say as churches. Churches in general, apart from the Pentecostals, are extremely cautious and apprehensive. *The American Ecclesiastical Review,* a publication of the Catholic University of America, has stated, "Whether another fad or a genuine religious experience, speaking in tongues, as St. Paul was aware, can be dangerous. Almost unheard of since the early days of the Church, glossolalia lends itself to abuse. Glossolalia may well, however superficially sincere, represent a psychopathological manifestation reminiscent of the Ouija board madness of the 1920's and the convulsionnaires of the cemetery of St. Médard in Paris, two centuries earlier. If it is indeed from God then ultimately the marks of authenticity will be present and discernible."[3]

Glossolalia could be called a countertide in religion, part of the restlessness and ferment moving at times in an opposite direction from that of the intellectual and social-action church.

In September, 1963, the Lutheran Church Council issued a

---

[3] Dom Patrick Granfield, Comment, *The American Ecclesiastical Review,* Washington, D.C., Vol. CXLIX, No. 5, 1963, p. 346.

statement on glossolalia, discussing some reported experiences and basing its own general attitude on the Biblical statements of Paul in his first epistle to the Corinthians.

The result was a flood of requests for clarification and guidance from Lutheran leaders in all parts of the country. The Council reported, "These requests come out of the bewilderment and confusion that result when some testify to personal blessings derived from speaking in tongues and others report dissension and conduct that reflects pride rather than love."

The Council then set forth its officially considered opinion:

"Recently some pastors in their teaching regarding the fullness of the Spirit have given the impression that it is attested to especially by speaking in tongues. This tends to confuse glossolalia with the fullness of the Spirit and to give it the status of a permanent possession . . .

"Many who profess to have the gift of speaking in tongues report that great blessings have been derived. These blessings are said to be found in the ease with which they can give themselves to worship in adoration, thanksgiving and prayer. It is worship in a posture where the activities of the conscious mind seem to be somewhat suspended for the moment. Any posture where the conscious mind is not in full control is more readily open to the influence of evil spirits as well as the Holy Spirit, and therein lies a danger. In the presence of potential blessing there is also potential danger and the possibility of much confusion . . ."[4]

The Church concluded this report by asking its pastors and congregations to adhere to three basic rules: There should be no promotion or practice of speaking in tongues at meetings where the congregation was gathered in the church or where they were acting together; there would be no instruction in the technique or practice of speaking in tongues; and those who professed to have the gift would "reserve its use for their devotional life."

[4] *Reports and Actions of the Second General Convention of the American Lutheran Church,* Oct. 21–27, 1964.

Glossolalia is part of the reaching out, exploring, searching that must stamp its mark on so much of today's religion, whether it be in healing or praying or speaking in tongues, or in the chanted hymns and prayers of the liturgical wing of the church. For liturgy itself is a phase of modern worship that is undergoing extensive renovations in the name of change and relevance.

SING, SINNER, SING

Renewal comes not only in the attitudes toward metaphysical issues, or the direction of outreach that religion takes. It comes also in the *modes* of outreach, in the service, the prayer, the prelude, the hymn of praise. Much of this is traditional, familiar, cherished. Much of it is also undergoing cataclysmic change.

The distinguished Catholic musicologist, liturgist, and associate editor of *America* magazine, Father C. J. McNaspy, in his book *Our Changing Liturgy,* relates an incident that occurred during Vatican Council II, on a morning when the liturgy was being celebrated by the Ethiopians in what he described as "their own rather piquant rite."

An Italian bishop, distressed at such unfamiliar ceremonies in the Holy See, exclaimed to his neighbor: "What a carnival!" The neighbor shrugged and commented, "Yes, Monsignore, but isn't the whole thing a carnival?"

By "the whole thing," Father McNaspy explains, he presumably meant St. Peter's, the Council, and the liturgy.

"The anecdote," Father McNaspy writes, "focuses on several

61

of the unresolved—perhaps never-to-be-resolved—tensions that are central to any liturgical discussion. What is the proper element of 'carnival' in liturgy or any celebration? When does culture become *Kitsch?* At what point does unity freeze into uniformity? To what extent does catholicity imply diversity? How popular should the mode of worship done by God's people actually be . . . ?"[1]

Nowhere is the problem of how fast and how far change should go more complex than in the question of liturgy. The song of songs—can it be modern, can it be jazz, can it be pop? Even at the altar of God?

Early in 1967, the Vatican announced that jazz masses were not to be conducted in Roman Catholic churches because they had not been properly or sufficiently developed. The door was not closed to the future, however; the Vatican announcement had the tone of a worried parent, willing to be modern but concerned about how far this ought to go.

But a musician who has composed an entire jazz mass for the Roman Catholic church asks: "Why should our music of joyful celebration not be as joyful as we are? Why should it be sad, doleful, dull and very often simply poor and ineffectual musical composition?"

In 1966, before the Vatican ban on the "jazz mass," hundreds of worshipers at a Roman Catholic church in New York's Harlem participated in what they called a joyous version of the Mass. This was a mass composed by Eddie Bonnmere, a brilliant musician and composer who teaches music in New York City public schools. His mass, entitled *Missa Hodierna* (Contemporary Mass), is dedicated to mothers, because, as he explains, "Mothers of the world so often have little recognition."

A strange mass to listen to, with tempos not usually associated with the wine and the breaking of the bread, it begins with the

---

[1] C. J. McNaspy, S. J., *Our Changing Liturgy,* New York: Hawthorn Books, 1966, p. 11.

words of a familiar song: "Sometimes I feel like a motherless child . . ."

But the tempo is not the slow, familiar one we know nor is the melody. It is jazz, lilting, swift-moving. And in the jazz tempo, the words themselves assume unexpected new meaning.

At Grace Episcopal Cathedral in San Francisco, a famous jazz musician brings a band of twenty other musicians to sound their brasses, drums and voices in the hot licks of praise to God. He has been brought there by the then Bishop Pike, who sits in the congregation to listen to what he describes as a "religious statement." The Very Rev. C. Julian Bartlett, dean of the cathedral, in introducing this jazz band leader and his music makers, declares: "Duke Ellington has been endowed by God with the gift of genius. He and his company of artists make an offering to God in this concert."[2]

At the Episcopal Washington National Cathedral, in November, 1966, an elaborate jazz communion was held with more than ten priests serving and assisting. Music was provided by folk singer and guitarist Robert Edwin and by the Joseph Newman Quartet—a jazz trumpeter, bass violist, pianist, and drummer. The service included "An Improvisation on the 150th Psalm," read by the Rev. Mr. Gensel, Lutheran pastor to the jazz community of New York City, a jazz gradual, and a jazz interlude before the communion.

There are some who consider this whole approach profane. Yet the other side has arguments to counter such charges. Here is the approach of the preacher and celebrant of the communion that day, the Right Rev. Daniel T. Corrigan, as recorded in the program for that Saturday afternoon service:

"In the early days of the Christian Church the altar was the table around which the family of Christ gathered to partake of the sacramental meal; it was customarily placed in the midst of

2 "Washington Worshipers Listen as Jazz Sings a 'New Song'." *The Lutheran*, Vol. 3, No. 21, Oct. 27, 1965, p. 38.

the congregation. At the time of the Reformation the Anglican Church harked back to this primitive usage. It translated the liturgy into the language of the people and returned the altar to a visibly central place. At this service the early practice is resumed. The very title of our Book of Common Prayer indicates the corporate nature of our worship. It is an act in which we unite around a common table. Here, as the Gospel declares, is Christ in our midst 'where two or three are gathered in his Name.' For after all it is the people themselves who are offering their lives, their work and faith to God in the Eucharist. Here unworthiness is healed and sinners are sanctified and God's blessing is bestowed on the whole company of believers."[3]

One might ask: Is this a profane approach to the table of the Lord? Or is meaning in the service heightened, as many of the jazz musicians and their followers claim, by recognition that the secular world is also valid as part of God's universe within the church walls and beyond? The church, as Duke Ellington is reported to have pointed out to one critic, is concerned with sinners and salvation.

Pastor Gensel believes that meaning in religion requires communication in the idiom of the age, the idiom of the people.

Early in his career, Pastor Gensel had a church on the upper West Side of Manhattan. In his community were many young jazz musicians. He came to know them and their families, he listened to the music and found it moving, valid, expressive. Sometimes at night when he talked with musicians, they asked him about God and faith. They also asked: But what about this music played and sung in churches? Did it have to be that bad? Too much "church music" was simply second-rate music, frayed melodies, repetitive, unimaginative, often meaningless either as music or faith. They were not the only ones to discover this:

---

[3] Program, Washington Cathedral, Mount Saint Alban, Washington, D.C., Saturday, Nov. 12, 1966.

Many churches have experts on music who know the difference between the good and the bad.

Pastor Gensel, becoming a full-fledged jazz "buff" himself, began to realize that two factors were at work. The first was the church's need for new music that could speak to average people in the idiom of the age, the popular, living idiom. And the second was the need of the jazz musicians themselves for concern and care. Too many people playing, singing, dancing were subjected to too many pressures, too many evils that could destroy them.

In 1962 the United Lutheran Church in America sponsored a three-day workshop on jazz and contemporary culture in a Greenwich Village nightclub called the Village Gate. Clergymen, musicians of all types, students, and jazz enthusiasts participated. Some of it was smoke and laughter and hot music. Some of it was solemn and concerned. A famed drummer and composer, Max Roach, told the participants that the church of our time "is obligated to come into the clubs where we work and save our young men from the things that can destroy them. Seek us out and teach us the moral values that can save us."[4]

Another musician, guitarist and composer Mundell Lowe, told the gathering that the public image of the jazz musician was associated with "streetwalkers and back-room dives."

Pastor Gensel explained how jazz music had originated in religion—in the spirituals of the Negro people. One day, he said, "the divorce that occurred when jazz moved out of the church and into the clubs would be reconciled."

In a subsequent interview in his New York apartment, black-haired, relaxed, in shirtsleeves, Gensel talked about what liturgy means to him.

"Music in its primitive form was almost all religious," he said.

---

[4] Press release, United Lutheran Church in America, March 1, 1962, p. 1.

"In ancient Greece it was so, and in Africa. Tribal music was music of prayer."

All this was modified and changed, he agreed, as time took the music out of the primitive stage, and out of religion, into the sophisticated melodies of New Orleans. But even in its sophistication, it was searching, articulating yearnings, hurts, needs.

The idea that the great churches of America, bastions of God and of conforming society, would break away from that conformity to accept the new folk-music beat was still, five years later, new and in many ways shocking to regular churchgoers.

The jazz musicians and the others who followed, came as individuals and in small groups, often with odd names, bringing their own music into the churches. In St. Mark's Church in Kingston, Ontario, a guitar player replaced the organ to accompany the congregation singing the hymns at special folk-music services on Sunday evenings.

Inaugurated in September, 1964, the services drew large gatherings, mostly of young people. The Rev. Roy Oswald, who started the programs in Ontario, states that the young people find the folk music more meaningful than standard hymns. To those who object to his innovations, Pastor Oswald poses the query: What proof do we have that God really prefers organ music in church?

The rhythms of the popular ballad singers have thus taken on unsuspected tones; the singing of people like Harry Belafonte and Pete Seeger are found to have religious content and concern.

In St. James's Episcopal Church on New York's Madison Avenue in April, 1967, a Sunday morning service included a folk-rock hymn session. The hymns were sung by a group from St. Paul's School in Concord, New Hampshire, who called themselves the "Drunken Lords."

The five young men, all wearing dark suits and white shirts, all carefully groomed, included three guitar players and one drummer. They drew a large gathering of youths, parents, children. They drew some who came to be shocked, who were startled to hear the Lord's Prayer and the *Kyrie Eleison* played on electric guitars and sung to the beat of a folk singer's drum.

One woman in the congregation declared that she felt she hadn't been to church at all. Another said that she wanted to forget what she had heard.

But the younger people delighted in the experience and crowded around the singers afterward.

Liturgy is the work of the people in making a church live, in making it effective as a route of communication between the created and the Creator.

In London, England, the world-famous church of St. Mary-le-Bow—the church of the Bow Bells in Cheapside—has developed a new avenue of reaching the world through dialogue with the world.

The dialogue is carried out through a device within the church itself—twin pulpits, with the clergyman in one, and in the other a spokesman from the world, who may be atheist or believer.

The Reverend Joseph McCulloch of St. Mary's explains that while the church was being rebuilt, he conceived the idea of twin pulpits as a way of making modern religion more meaningful and exciting to the people, the world, believing or nonbelieving.

Writing in *New Christian Magazine,* Father McCulloch declared:

"My hunch was that, at the very least, if there were two speakers and they were visibly on equal terms, people of an inquiring mind might want to listen to their conversation, and judge for themselves in which direction the truth lay. Hence the importance of the two identical pulpits, from which two people could discuss any matter under the sun, with difference admittedly, but without inequality. I also insisted on providing movable chairs instead of fixed pews. My aim was to replace the fixed lecture-hall pattern of the church with one which was seen to permit of flexibility, free enquiry and the open mind."[5]

In the first weeks, only clergymen participated in the dialogues. Then the second pulpit was opened to all who seemed to have something of importance to say.

Agreeing that one pulpit should always have a clergyman speaking for the church, Father McCulloch weighed carefully who should be in the other. He was soon led, he states, to the obvious answer. They should be people who had already gained a hearing before the world.

"They should include writers, broadcasters, stage and screen personalities, scientists, musicians, architects, politicians, indeed any who were already acknowledged 'communicators,' in any of the various departments of modern living."[6]

The dialogues, which have covered an almost unlimited range of topics, have drawn tremendous crowds and have started a new liturgical development that has already spread to a number of other churches. Father McCulloch reports that when a particular dialogue has been unusually stimulating, "knots of people are to be seen afterwards in Cheapside, continuing the discussion . . ."

At St. Mark's in the Bowery, in New York, numerous dramatic plays have been staged over the years by Ralph Cook, lay minister to the arts at St. Mark's, under the guidance of the pastor, the Rev. Michael Allen.

Much praised and equally denounced for its unique program, St. Mark's exemplifies the "new religion" in action. The Rev. Allen, for example, grew up in an agnostic-atheistic Greenwich Village atmosphere, the son of the noted reporter-writer, Jay Allen. He himself became a journalist. During an interview with former Bishop James Pike, Allen began to glimpse in his mind a new kind of religion, one that lived by meanings rather than

---

[5] Rev. Joseph McCulloch, "Dialogue with the World," *New Christian Magazine,* November, 1966, p. 8.
[6] *Ibid.,* p. 8.

forms. He entered the seminary to begin study for the Episcopal priesthood without even having been confirmed.

As the pastor of St. Mark's, he has conducted a church that reaches out to all the parish. To Allen the church belongs to the parish and everyone living in it, regardless of his or her faith or lack of it. St. Mark's communion, in fact, is open to all.

Ralph Cook himself was agnostic; he believed in something beyond himself but was not sure what. Always interested in the theater, he found himself, after a brief Hollywood career, work-ing in a Village café to help support his children by a marriage that had ended in divorce. Sometimes, on days when he had visiting rights with the children, he would take them to St. Mark's nursery school. One day, waiting for them, he aimlessly went into the church.

Allen was speaking from the pulpit. Cook listened and was amazed. This was language not usually associated with pulpits but with human beings. He visited the church again; he came to know Father Allen. He debated and argued religion and theol-ogy with him; finally he allowed himself to be baptized—at the same time as his children—and later he entered confirmation classes. Gradually, in the course of this study, he began to realize what true submission to God really meant. "If you are an atheist, then you yourself have to be God. But this is foolishness; we aren't God. And, when we come to realize this, we realize that we can submit to Him willingly and gladly, and in submitting to His love, we find that we ourselves are free."

As an actor and director, Cook describes himself and his experience in theatrical terms:

"In a successful production, the participants—the actors, playwright, director, designers—all submit to the play, and it is in this submission that they and the play achieve their reality and meaning.

"The submission at the altar is like a performer in a play, only the stage is much larger, the consequences are far greater. The theater and all the creative arts are a reiteration of what happens in the Eucharist."

Many of the plays that have been produced—they total some threescore at this writing—have dealt with "way-out" topics. Many are concerned with sex problems, many speak in the language of the streets and the gutters and brothels—and all of this is set forth on the stage of the St. Mark's workshop theater.

Cook declares that in his view such plays, written by talented young playwrights in the community, are a form of confession for the community. Christianity tells us to lay our sins at the altar in Christ's church. Is the drama that seems so vulgar, so full of human filth, not in fact another way of putting this sinning at the altar? "Is it not," Cook asks, "a cry for forgiveness?"

In the spring of 1966, in the Annandale Methodist Church, Annandale, Virginia, the minister and two jazz musicians, Howard McGhee on the trumpet and Roger Kellaway on the piano, held a series of worship services.

So moved was one young woman at the sense of joy that permeated the services that she wrote down her reactions as she listened to the music. The spontaneous words of that unidentified young worshiper have a quality of fervor that seems to go back to the first days of the church:

"Listen to that music and listen to him. That's pure joy and love for something he can't explain or understand—yet he found one thing that he can put his body and soul into. Every service has been different—I'll bet that guy feels so deeply about something . . . Maybe his God is himself and his piano—but that faith is so deep in this man that in itself is more than all the pitched and harmonized noise that a whole congregation of 'habitual worshipers' can raise up to any old man with a long white beard on a golden throne and a white cloud. This can really prove something to the individual—How well do you worship or do you worship without a planned order? Can you see God in different forms beside the way? I feel like I've been washed by a spring shower and cooled by a summer breeze. Sound queer? It feels queer! Church can become so stuffy—I asked once to find an identity with God that few had—I think I've found a part of it without knowing I had it all the time."[7]

---

[7] The Jazz Worship Service, New Conception Worship, a prayer prepared for a course in the Sociology of Religion, Brooklyn College, Spring, 1966, by Allan Repper, p. 4.

ESP: HIGHWAY TO THE SOUL

Among the issues facing organized religions today is what to do about metaphysical developments that gain substantial acceptance in areas generally opposed to religion. Extrasensory perception (ESP) is a candidate in this field.

By ESP is meant episodes of spontaneous knowing, or information an individual obtains or transmits to others by channels other than the physical senses.

It was Dr. J. B. Rhine, investigator of extrasensory perception, who reportedly brought "parapsychology" to the English language as a translation of a German word for the new science that explores experience beyond the five senses.

Had Dr. Rhine lived a few centuries ago in the American colonies or in England, he might well have been burned as a male witch. In Spain during the Inquisition, church authorities would have sentenced him to death for being in league with Satan.

For many centuries formal religion has stood as guardian against the perils, real or imagined, that reside in spiritualism, mind reading, fortune-telling, and all forms of the occult. Part of the fear was based on the undeniably fraudulent character of many who practiced these arts. Part arose because so much in religion involves claims of miraculous events, most of which can never be either proved or disproved factually. Religious authorities also warn against the possibility of Satan's deceiving the individual in such episodes.

But today members of all faiths, including clergymen, have been quietly investigating what lies beyond the opening doors of parapsychology.

Serious religious groups also are beginning to examine the results of Dr. Rhine's work, as well as that of others of similar purpose.

At centers such as Wainwright House in Rye, New York, devoted to exploration of all aspects of modern faith and paranormal experience, men of science, psychology, and religion have met on many occasions to examine these questions.

Religious concern about Dr. Rhine's investigations into extrasensory perception becomes particularly important because Dr. Rhine has taken the subject away from gypsies and boardwalk fortune-tellers and has given a stamp of tentative scientific verification to thousands of psychic episodes involving average individuals. With more and more colleges and universities exploring or beginning to explore such phenomena, organized religion is no longer able to dismiss lightly their possible implications.

One result has been confusion and ambivalence of attitude. No one is any longer sure where psychic truth ends and the superstitious, the fraudulent—or, as some insist, the Satanic—begins. The fact that the power on which ESP depends is thus far almost totally unidentified makes even the most authentic case of ESP at least questionable. Even where an experience itself may be accepted as apparently valid, the interpretation usually allows several points of view.

Dr. Rhine seeks answers to the nature of existence and cognition. In effect, he asks: Is it possible that there is no difference in kind between what we call normal and what we call paranormal, that the psychic substance is merely a higher form of the material substance, energy, or force? Is each in its own way indestructible?

Organized religion is sharply divided on these questions. Church intellectuals generally shy away from anything verging on the "supernatural." Fundamentalists accept the miraculous of the past but view with suspicion modern approaches that might plunge into the demonic. Because ESP deals primarily with the human mind, with episodes that appear solidly bound to this earth, it represents at present a kind of theological no-man's-land between the spiritual and the material.

Both within and outside the church we find those who speak and write of ESP as an accepted fact. A leading theologian of the Roman Catholic faith, Father Reginald Omez, in his book *Psychical Phenomena,* affirms the conclusion that Rhine's experiments with cards and controlled testing have established beyond question that telepathy and clairvoyance exist. Father Omez writes:

"Once the existence of extrasensory perception was proved, the parapsychologists strove to find an explanation. What is the nature of this perception? What are its vectors or vehicles, what organs transmit or receive it? . . .

"Contemporary parapsychologists admit that the psi-function is probably universal. It is easy to see, indeed, that the phenomena of telepathy, second sight, vertical presentiments and so on occur among people of very different gifts and temperaments.

"Moreover, telepathic perceptions can be observed in a high degree of development among animals; dogs, for instance, who show it not only in connection with man, but with their fellows whose sufferings, anxieties or appeals for help they perceive from great distances.

"We can therefore assert that these phenomena do not seem to be exclusively reserved to certain human beings, highly gifted, supersensitive or subjected to the influence of alien beings. Paranormal cognition, as found in all human individuals and in at least a very large number of animals, is a natural thing."[1]

I have quoted Father Omez' carefully thought-out exposition because it clarifies, I believe, the important reason that many organized religions shy away from telepathy and its implications. For what he is talking about is essentially a force, and its nature, as he describes it, is seemingly physical and materialistic, rather than spiritual. The intuitional force, in the eyes of Father Omez, is something that the new science of parapsychology is in the process of exploring. Religion he sees as something totally different; religion is not talking to us in terms of what this force may or may not be, but in terms of universal, timeless, and changeless truth.

In defense of the church's position on scientific investigations, Father Omez contends that the church does not oppose and has not opposed scientific discoveries or investigations even when they seem to contradict theological positions long held by the churches. What is objected to (here he is speaking solely of the Roman Catholic official objection) is the publication or spreading of statements that are purely hypothetical and conjectural and remain to be proven. One could debate at length with Father Omez on this defense of the church authorities and the theory of "censored until proven true."

It is certainly not unnatural that ministers of the gospel, dealing often, of necessity, with the supernatural, should experience episodes themselves, whether or not the church frowns. Nor could the pastor turn from an experience merely because it touches on the supernatural. A Methodist minister, with whom I discussed the fear of some clergymen that ESP may involve them with the demonic, declared, "But if we could establish scientifi-

---

[1] Reginald Omez, O. P., *Psychical Phenomena*, translated from the French by Renée Haynes. New York: Hawthorn Books, 1958, pp. 117–118.

cally that demons exist—wouldn't that also establish the reality of the non-fallen angels as well?"

Unlike the church, Dr. Rhine is not hampered by taboos and traditions. He states quite baldly in *The Reach of the Mind* that the answer to the question of whether man is solely physical or partly spiritual or "extraphysical" is that man is in part spiritual. He states for the record: "There now is evidence that such an extraphysical factor exists in man."[2]

A widely reported incident occurred some years ago in the First Methodist Church of Red Bank, New Jersey, several days after a train wreck in nearby Woodbridge in which many persons were killed or hurt. One of the severely injured was Robert Stout, a member of the church. On Sunday morning, the pastor, the Rev. Roger J. Squires, spoke of the concern all felt for him, of the fact that he had been in a coma and was to have brain surgery that morning.

In the midst of the service the pastor, acting on a spontaneous impulse, went down into the aisle and fell on his knees, surrounded by the congregation. Together they prayed for Stout's life.

Later they learned that at the precise moment they prayed, Stout was being wheeled to the operating room, when one of the attendants noticed that he had opened his eyes and lifted his head. As a result, the operation was canceled. Stout recovered within a matter of days without surgery.

The facts in the case are not questioned; they have been attested to by many individuals, and the story was published in *Reader's Digest* after thorough investigation. From the supernatural religious point of view, it was the working of God, a seemingly miraculous intervention.

The parapsychologist, on the other hand, would have to raise certain questions: Was the pastor's impulse to do something

---

[2] J. B. Rhine, *The Reach of the Mind,* New York: William Sloane Associates, Inc., 1947, p. 206.

totally different from usual church procedures—praying in the center aisle rather than from the pulpit—a result of a specific impulse from God, or was it an extrasensory perception of what was at that moment happening in the hospital? Is there also the possibility that the combined force of the congregation and the pastor in prayer could itself become the psi-factor, the wavelength impulse that awakened the man.

Extrasensory perception may well be one of the forces man has still to learn to understand and use. Just as the churches are now deeply involved in investigation of healing and have found that a partnership of medical, psychological, and spiritual disciplines is a highly effective "team" for helping mankind, so they may find that a similar probing of ESP may bring us closer to understanding what at present remains a mystery to both religion and science.

Interweavings of science and religion are by now familiar phenomena of man's quest for truth. An interesting example of this is found in the relationship of Dr. Elwood Worcester, who, as related earlier, brought religious healing into the Episcopal Church, and Dr. Rhine, who more than any other man has helped to make extrasensory perception and other parapsychological research respectable in American universities.

As an individual, Dr. Worcester was seriously concerned with all varieties of psychic phenomena. He was disturbed by the sad state into which American psychic research had fallen after the tempestuous and controversial mediumship of a woman named Minna Crandon, whose husband was a Boston surgeon. The American Society of Psychic Research backed her mediumship and thereby lost face with much of a doubting public. Dr. Worcester—who did not support Mrs. Crandon's achievements as a medium—helped to form the Boston Society of Psychic Research and to bring into it leaders in intellectual life. Among these was Professor William MacDougall, noted psychologist and head of the psychology department of Harvard University. During the 1920's, under his direction, many experiments in telepathy were conducted, with varying attempts at controlled conditions.

Historically, this era marked the beginning of twentieth-century scientific objectivity on all fronts, including that of religion. Old attitudes had to be reexamined, old nonsense erased, old falsehoods exploded, old taboos lifted. It was no longer superstition for its own sake, or antisuperstition for its own sake. It was the beginning of a new awareness that religious man had a divine obligation to search out the facts.

In correspondence with a young Chicago botanist in whose work he had become interested, Professor MacDougall hinted at this cosmic possibility as one reason for launching new research under incorruptible investigators.

The young botanist was Rhine, who insisted both then and later that his approach was not religious but exclusively scientific. The fact that he had once thought of going into the ministry had no effect upon his attitude, he asserted repeatedly. Nor did it influence his early attitudes when he and his wife, also a botanist, began their experiments in psychic research. Dr. Rhine certainly could not then be classified as a churchgoer, although his wife Louisa always had closer ties to basic formal religious concepts than her husband. He joined MacDougall at Harvard as a research assistant and the following year went with him to Duke University. It was at Duke that Rhine began his first fully controlled investigations of the ESP factor in the transference of thought.

Here we see the direct link between the healing techniques developed by Dr. Worcester, with clergy and ministers working together, and the scientific investigation of telepathy, with which Worcester and his friend MacDougall, and later Dr. Rhine, were also concerned.

One of Rhine's most conclusive early cases, perhaps by coincidence, involved a student at Duke who came from a background of clairvoyant interests and was himself studying for the ministry. The young man was put through hundreds of Dr. Rhine's "card guessing" tests. These widely known tests use cards with five basic designs—star, square, circle, wave, and cross; the deck is made up of five cards of each design. Mechanical shuffling insures that cards are stacked solely by chance.

The divinity student was one of the highest scorers in months of testing. In the autumn of 1933, the following experiment occurred:

"The subject, H. P., was located in a building 100 yards away from that in which the experimenter with the target cards was situated. A series of twelve runs through the pack of cards was conducted by my assistant, Mr. J. G. Pratt, a graduate student in psychology at the time. The two men worked with synchronized watches; Pratt shuffled the cards just prior to the test and placed them, one at a time, face down in the center of the table for one minute before removal. In this way the 300-trial test of clairvoyance was completed at the rate of fifty trials per day for six days. The results were independently checked from the duplicate records kept by both men. H. P. was found to have averaged 9.9 hits per run for twenty-five trials as against 5.0 to be expected from chance. The odds against chance producing so high a score are of the order of a *hundred trillions to one*."[3]

One may ask what relationship such card games have to religion? The answer can only be that they provide materialistic but valid techniques of investigation into the whole field of ESP.

There exists a wealth of uncontrolled but still largely verifiable ESP episodes. Many of these instances involve moments of catastrophe, near-catastrophe, danger, or death.

A case was reported to the author some years ago by a close friend, the late Mrs. Marian Robb, former nurse at New York's Harkness Pavilion and widow of a renowned Baltimore gynecolo-

---

[3] Guildhall Lectures, Manchester, England: Granada Television, 1965, p. 18.

gist. Among her friends was a man who had been for many years president of a great American insurance firm. Both were in late middle age; they had known each other for a long time. Several times he had told her: "Don't worry, my dear. If anything happens to me, I will let you know myself."

Having lost her husband years before, Mrs. Robb lived alone in a large house in Point Pleasant, New Jersey. One night, about one-thirty A.M., her doorbell rang. When she went to answer it no one was there. She went back to bed. This was repeated several times, but there was never anyone at the door. Finally it became so annoying that she called the police, on the theory that it might be some youths playing pranks.

Police investigating found nothing—no sign of young culprits on the street, nothing wrong with the bell. It did not ring while they were there except when they pressed it, and it stopped when they stopped pressing it.

When they left, the bell began to ring again. Several times Mrs. Robb answered, but there was no one. At seven o'clock in the morning it rang for the last time.

Less than an hour later, according to her story, she received word by telephone that her friend had died that morning—at approximately seven o'clock.

Such cases appear to happen most often in times of crisis and between people who have close bonds. Husbands and wives, miles apart, will know when something of a serious nature has occurred. Sometimes the word comes unbidden, frightening. Dr. Rhine cites a case in which a professor at Duke received a cable from overseas. A young man whose parents were friends of the professor's had died suddenly abroad. Would the professor break this tragic news to the parents? But when the professor went to the father, the father revealed that he already knew, that his wife had told him three days earlier—the actual day on which the son had died! The father could not explain how she could have known; "She just knew," he said.

Most of us have had some such personal experience. One

night Helen, my sister, called to tell me her husband was in a coma, apparently from shock. My wife and I hurried to the hospital in Queens, New York. It was bitter winter weather, and icy sleet was coating the streets dangerously. Several times our cab driver lost his way. Every delay only heightened our concern. Then suddenly, as the car sped along Queens Boulevard, all my tension seemed to disappear. I felt quite calm. "It doesn't matter now," I said, "Joe is dead."

I did not know how I knew this; I knew only that I had to say it—dreadful as it was to say. I knew also that it was true. There was no question, no element of doubt.

We reached a main intersection. Ahead was a large lighted advertising sign with a clock. The clock said ten minutes past eight.

When finally we reached the hospital and asked for my brother-in-law, the man behind the desk said, "You know that he died, don't you?"

I said, "Yes, I know." And I added, "What was the time, can you tell me?"

"It was just after eight o'clock."

In the town of Killingworth, Connecticut, in the spring of 1967, news stories were carried locally and on the wires of the Associated Press telling of a resident who awoke in terror from a nightmare in which one of her sisters appeared to be suddenly dangerously ill. So real was the dream that the woman got out of bed and tried to reach her sisters' home by phone.

At first there was no answer. When finally she reached them, she learned that someone nearby had smelled smoke and turned in an alarm. Otherwise, all four sisters would have been asphyxiated from a fire that had broken out as they slept.

Was it merely a coincidence—the dream, the telephone call, the fire? Or was it actually an example of the "psi" force at work? Most of the people in Killingworth will tell you it was the latter.

More and more the church is being compelled to accept a role in what many of its own leaders consider to be the credulous and superstitious. And it appears also, to some of those concerned about the new "way-out" aspects of religion, that both the acceptance and doubts are vital in the church of our times. Must not the modern church, in any case, begin helping pastors and seminarians through training seminars, to understand the controversial aspects of ESP metaphysics—if only to enable them to answer questions out of sound and well-grounded information?

Is there an active force of mind that can probe the past—even the future—that can cross time and space?

PROPHECY AND PRECOGNITION

If ESP and its relationship to religion raise difficult questions, even more troublesome are the areas of prophecy and precognition. Dr. Rhine's "psi" factor could well be a purely physical force. But how could such a force cross a time-dimension into the future? And what is the relationship to religion?

The church was built by its prophets, but the term prophet as used biblically has little crystal-ball connotation. Biblical prophets were not fortune-tellers but spoke of things God revealed to them for the direction of man. Harper's *Bible Dictionary* asserts that biblical prophecy is not concerned "primarily with foretelling future events, in the sense in which one speaks of a weather prophet or a financial forecaster. It deals rather with *forth*telling the intuitively felt will of God for a specific situation in the life of an individual or a nation. . . ."[1]

The same source also points out that the Hebrew word "prophet" means literally "one who speaks for another." Biblical

---

[1] Madeleine S. and J. Lane Miller, *Harper's Bible Dictionary*. New York: Harper and Bros., 1952, 1954, 1955, p. 582.

prophets spoke to the people for God, to point the way to true religion and the shunning of evil. Where they spoke of the future, it was to warn that the sin of today could be found in the evil of tomorrow, and that the good sown today is reaped in the bounty to come.

So-called precognition of actual future events is a far different and more dangerous area. It is an area of the paranormal in which great harm can be done. Unlike spiritual healing—in which churches have a safeguard in their insistence that such therapy must be given in cooperation with medical authorities—there is no check on where fortune-telling begins or ends.

Religious interpretation of prophecy today must begin on a basis of the facts. Question one: Did the thing really happen as claimed? Question two: What meaning can we give to it, if it did occur as presented? And finally: What relationship does all of this have to the religious truth? To God acting in our lives.

The individual, particularly the religious individual, who finds himself caught in the web of an apparent psychic gift, is usually bewildered—very often frightened. A young woman known to the author who was seemingly gifted with psychic precognition would say things whose meaning she herself did not comprehend; sometimes they would refer to events that later actually happened.

If there is no psychic gift at all, if precognition is all guesswork, coincidence, or fraud, or if psychic gifts are associated only with demonic forces and therefore always perilous, the church, in the view of many of its own members, ought to speak out unequivocally on what these things mean today.

I have talked with many pastors, for example, who, while claiming no special psychic gift, nevertheless appear to develop powers of understanding and reaching forth beyond the normal ability. The pastor of a suburban church told me of how, when he first took over the church, it was in a very poor state physically, with plaster falling off the walls, the condition of the altar a disgrace, so also the pews and the vestry. With what spare funds they had available, they "made do" to carry on the worship of God.

"We prayed about the situation," he told me, "but then quite suddenly, I knew we would have an answer. I was not guessing. I knew."

How could he know that a man was going to die and leave the church a substantial sum, sufficient to renovate the entire building? The man was a complete stranger to him and to the church, an agnostic who put no trust in God.

A famous American writer and lecturer awoke one day with a vivid dream burned into his mind. In his dream he had seen his wife standing almost nude in a pool of blood. The stench of the blood was strong in his nostrils. Something or someone was hurt and needed help. And the blood had to be cleaned up. Approximately nine hours later, when he returned home from work, he walked into a scene of crisis. The kitchen was covered with blood exactly as he had pictured it in his dream. His wife, also covered with blood, stood in the midst of this scene, dressed only in a slip. The writer learned that the family dog had been run over and injured. The details of the dream and the details of the scene when the bleeding dog was brought in were the same. The dog later recovered.

This precognitive dream I recount from vivid personal recollection; the author was my father, Fulton Oursler. Although he later became a Roman Catholic convert, he remained convinced of these and other episodes in his own experience.

Ruth Montgomery, well-known psychic writer, in 1967 wrote a magazine article—later reprinted in *Reader's Digest*—recounting psychic experiences of her friends in Washington and elsewhere. These episodes involved premonitions of events that were to happen—or were in the process of happening. One involved the wife of the American war hero, Gen. Nathan F. Twining, during a period when he was missing at sea following a crash.

Mrs. Twining—ten thousand miles away—saw her husband at the foot of her bed. Later, after his rescue, knowing nothing about her experience, he reported to her that he had seen her before him just before the plane crashed.

Lists of such experiences run into the tens of thousands. They are not a part of the past, they are not remnants out of the middle ages of ignorance and superstition. They are a part of our current space-age life.

A leading Catholic theologian and philosopher, Dr. Alois Wiesinger, declares in the introduction to his book *Occult Phenomena:*

"Explanations of occultism are as varied as they are numerous; the materialists seek to explain it in terms of matter and its movements, by a theory of 'waves,' the exact nature of which is not yet known. Others believe that we are dealing with reappearances of the dead, with 'rebirths,' or with a 'perispirit' which is not truly either spirit or body but is what is called an astral body. The majority of learned Christians fall back on the devil, who is supposed in these cases to misuse human powers and so to deceive us. Admittedly they try increasingly to ascribe as many of these phenomena as possible to natural powers. So far, however, they do not appear to have arrived at a satisfactory explanation."[2]

Catholic writers are among the leaders in exploring and reporting on the meaning of occult and supernatural events, including the activities of clairvoyants who foretell the future. Yet among Catholics themselves, there is no unanimity of opinion.

Laboratory tests by Dr. Rhine and other investigators have probed the possibility of telepathically identifying not merely the turned-up card that someone is looking at (and presumably televising mentally to the subject) but the next card, the card waiting face down. On this basis, in an astronomical number of

---

[2] Alois Wiesinger, *Occult Phenomena,* translated by Brian Battershaw. Westminster, Maryland: The Newman Press, 1957, p. viii.

cases, gifted individuals have tested out far beyond the chance level.

Father Omez declares in *Psychical Phenomena*, on the subject of predictions of this character, probing the edges of the future with no basis in the known present: "The future remains a mystery, unsolved—and in all probability insoluble—by both philosophy and science.

"Must it not be faced that only the hypothesis that entities foreign to man are at work can make sense of the numerous authentic instances of precognition and knowledge of the future?"[3]

Renée Haynes, Father Omez' translator, appended a footnote as follows:

"Not unless one is prepared to admit that these entities intervene on behalf of animals as well as human beings, and moreover exert themselves through thousands of card experiments to help the percipient guess one card ahead of that being proposed for their attention. The necessity of rethinking our ideas about the nature of time seems a more probable explanation."[4]

There are cogent reasons for the concern of modern church authorities with so-called parapsychological phenomena. The uncertainties of our age leave areas in which individuals need guidance, particularly the individual drawn into a net of new superstition, new techniques of mind-influencing, of will-domination, mastery of others, new ways to get what you want or to keep others from achieving their goals.

Records indicate that millions of churchgoers also believe in astrological predictions. It is reported that leading officials in the United States government follow the astrological charts. Hundreds of daily and weekly papers carry regular columns dealing with the stars and what they portend, side by side with columns

---

3 Reginald Omez, O. P., *Psychical Phenomena*, translated from the French by Renée Haynes. New York: Hawthorn Books, 1952, p. 124.

4 *Ibid.*, p. 124, footnote.

by physicians advising on health and political authorities analyzing world events.

One of the best-selling books of the 1960's, first published in 1965, was Ruth Montgomery's *A Gift of Prophecy,* about Jeanne Dixon, who predicted President John F. Kennedy's assassination.

There are some disturbing implications in this book. Mrs. Dixon's use of a crystal ball, for example, raises questions: It seems so solid an object with which to move into the metaphysical. And its use is beclouded by so much ancient association with the gypsy, the carnival, the magic show. She does not use it all the time, nor does she give it the highest role in her precognitions, which come often with no material aid whatever. But because she says plainly, and obviously believes deeply, that her gift of prophecy is from God, one must ask: Is the crystal ball with its assorted connotations a proper avenue for such a gift? Must God—indeed, would God—disclose His sacred will through such a means?

It would be possible to be disturbed by the political connotations of some of the predictions. With a little less reliance on psychic forces and a little more on local informants, might she be, in some of her more earthy prognostications, simply another political pundit?

The book quotes her as saying in a private conversation with the late President Franklin D. Roosevelt that our own racial situation would be a greater problem than our relations with Russia.

"The White House must not pamper the coloured people but rather help them to help themselves.

"Mr. President, these are not my thoughts, they come through channels from another sphere. The will of humanity does not change the will of God. The racial situation will not be solved before 1980."[5]

---

[5] Ruth Montgomery, *A Gift of Prophecy, the Phenomenal Jeanne Dixon.* New York: Bantam Books, 1966, p. 50.

We have the right to ask: What does she mean by "the will of God" in this situation? Was slavery, over which we fought one of the bloodiest wars in history, the will of God—or an unconscionable and un-Christian evil? Was the unspeakably brutal murder of three innocent human beings at a place called Philadelphia, Mississippi, the will of God? Was the assassination of Martin Luther King, Jr., the will of God?

One can be certain Mrs. Dixon meant nothing of the kind. But there is a vast difference between a psychic predicting the future correctly or incorrectly—and a psychic correctly or incorrectly seeking to establish her prophecy as the will of God.

Mrs. Dixon has every right to use her gift to the best of her abilities. I am entirely certain that she does just that, and seeks only to achieve good: warning, advising, guiding, helping. It is not to criticize that I have dwelt at length on her work. It is rather to point up places where one may differ as to what is happening and what is implied.

The whole field of precognition, as well as ESP, holds a new position today in the world. It is reported that the Russians have done research in depth in these fields, but with no connotation that a Supreme Creator plays any role. Thus, in both officially atheistic Russia and deistic America, paranormal communications are investigated outside of the religious realm.

Churches no longer condemn out of hand the paranormal, the psychic, the seer. But they warn—as Jesus warned—of the perils of those who do wonders but are not truly what they pretend. This is the modern predicament of the church: it cannot wholly accept, nor can it entirely reject.

Secular investigations of precognate experiences present a possibility of potential breakthrough and already are forcing theologians to speak softly, to hedge just a little in dealing with so-called sorcery, fortune-telling, and the like. Seminars on ESP and similar subjects have been held in Methodist and Episcopal churches, in conjunction with healing clinics and investigations of psychic therapy.

The church has its role also—if only in the protection of its members in this admittedly difficult and often equivocal area.

The theologian Paul Tillich essentially dismisses as "nonreligious" what he defines as "occult mysticism." Whether it is valid or not he refuses to debate, on the ground that it is as difficult to disprove occult experience as to prove it. And here he insists, with his usual oblique and even poetic clarity: "On this point it may be said that what religion means—that is the divine—is the absolutely hidden, that which transcends all experience, including occult experience. In the presence of the eternal even the occult is temporal, this-worldly, finite. In and of itself the occult sphere has no religious meaning. Like the world of experience it is subject to the judgment of the eternal, and it is like the former also in that it may serve to veil the eternal."[6]

But what may lie hidden in the occult may be as perilous as a time bomb in the choir loft.

There is no longer time merely to say: Leave it alone, it is dangerous. Certain groups in modern religion—Wainwright House in Rye, New York, as one example, and the national group known as Spiritual Frontiers as another—are exploring these fields. So are Dr. Rhine and his followers, in and out of the church.

The time has surely arrived for up-dated, hard-truth answers by religion as well as by the laity. And there are clear indications that today's church is accepting—and beginning to investigate objectively—the paranormal challenge.

---

[6] Paul Tillich, *The Religious Situation,* translated by H. Richard Niebuhr. New York: Meridian Books, Inc., 1962, p. 166.

CHAPTER X

DEVILS AND DRUMS

Millions believe in the existence not only of a personal God but also of a personal demon. The reality of Satan as an entity and the literal truth of the predictions of the Book of Revelations are accepted by virtually all the Pentecostal congregations, by the Seventh Day Adventists, by many Baptists, and by others who take the Bible literally. Belief in the existence of a personal devil is also fundamental in Roman Catholicism.

An important if largely inarticulated movement within the modern church, however, is the countertide *against* the personification of evil in an entity we call a devil. Thus, while the orthodox commitment to the idea of a real devil remains, intellectuals retreat from full acceptance; the demon becomes merely "demonic," generalized rather than personalized. If one judges solely by reading modern theological literature, or by examination of the general tenets of modern religion, one becomes impressed with the devil's role largely by the absence of reference to him or his alleged associates.

In some measure, the modern church finds itself in an equivocal position regarding questions of heaven and hell, devils and angels, good and evil. Satan is no longer a popular field of discussion or a Sunday sermon subject. "Hell fire" religion has become something of an embarrassment to modern religionists.

The possibility of an actual fiery hell somewhere "down there" is as difficult to defend today as that of a demon with tail and horns tending infernal furnaces. But defenders of such bizarre concepts still can be found.

Bishop Pike, however, told this writer that, in his view, if there were a literal hell, Jesus would be there tending the needs and sufferings of the damned. All the good people would come down from heaven to hell, he said, to perform works of Christian charity. "And God himself would get lonely and go down to hell to join with the others."

Not everyone, of course, would be in accord with such a jolting theological view. But it does indicate the change in thinking among many priests and pastors of our time. In some instances, the character of the devil and of hell are reinterpreted in terms of what churchgoers and nonchurchgoers create in this world. The good and evil are here and now, in what we do or fail to do. Hell becomes the flames we ourselves help to kindle.

This does not imply that modern religion is no longer concerned with evil; it means only that ancient ideas about demonology have been largely obliterated from advanced theological thinking. What remains is the empirical approach, the examination of evil in action in the world. The eschatological concerns of religion follow the teachings and interpretations of Paul Tillich, Karl Barth, Dietrich Bonhoeffer, Martin Buber, and others, to whom even the ultimates are endowed with a flexibility that mirrors the same flexibility in the teachings of Christ.

Even evil, these religious authorities appear to agree, is relative; even Satan assumes a degree of ambivalence. Does the pain that warns the individual to see his doctor come from heaven or hell? Were the demons whom Jesus drove out of the afflicted, as related in the synoptic gospels, actual physical beings, or were they the tormented totality of dislocations, disease, mental and emotional disorders?

Jesus speaks of the devil as a liar; Christian Science interprets this and similar statements by Jesus as proof that evil has no reality, that it is a human error, a misinterpretation of the universe.

In the gospels, Jesus gives glimpses of his technique of dealing with evil, sickness, trouble. In one instance he reveals to his disciples a fragment of his own metaphysical process when, after healing the boy with the falling-down sickness (apparently epilepsy), he declares, "Howbeit this kind goeth not out but by prayer and fasting."[1]

And here we find a paradox. Jesus speaks about the need of much fasting and prayer, but he himself had done no fasting or long prayer for this particular case. One must assume, then, that he was speaking of what was required for individuals of lesser power. He speaks of "this kind" and perhaps again invokes a meaning beyond the meaning, as if he appended an unuttered footnote: Demons, if you will, or in whatever terms you understand, *evil of this kind* comes out slow and hard.

Whatever the nature of the devil, whether entity or not, Jesus makes it clear that a counterpower within ourselves is important in dealing with the demonic. And to Jesus the demonic is referred to almost always in terms of falsehood. The liar, the murderer, who abides not in the truth. You shall know the truth and it shall make you free—from what? From the liar, the fallen angel, the demonic. Within ourselves, in our fasting and prayer to God we drive out the deceiver, the delusion of evil. But if it is totally false, where does religion find the reality of Satan?

The question of the nature of the beast has implications more elusive than the shape of the devil's tail or the size of his horns. Is

---

[1] Matthew XVII:21.

there any absolute evil? Are there degrees of right and wrong, heaven and hell, sin and not-sin, angels and devils? Was Hitler a paranoiac demon or a misdirected Germanic patriot? Is every lie evil, every truth good? Bonhoeffer himself, one of the victims of Hitler's monstrous murder camps, declares in one of his most powerful paragraphs:

"From the principle of truthfulness Kant draws the grotesque conclusion that I must even return an honest 'yes' to the enquiry of the murderer who breaks into my house and asks whether my friend whom he is pursuing has taken refuge there; in such a case self-righteousness of conscience has become outrageous presumption and blocks the path of responsible action. Responsibility is the total and realistic response of man to the claim of God and of our neighbour; but this example shows in its true light how the response of a conscience which is bound by principles is only a partial one. If I refuse to incur guilt against the principle of truthfulness for the sake of my friend (for it is only the self-righteously law-abiding conscience which will pretend that, in fact, no lie is involved), if, in other words, I refuse to bear guilt for charity's sake, then my action is in contradiction to my responsibility which has its foundation in reality. Here again it is precisely in the responsible acceptance of guilt that a conscience which is bound solely to Christ will best prove its innocence."[2]

To Bonhoeffer, the gist of the matter is not the words with which we describe evil, or the metaphysical explanation, but our own response to humanity itself.

No simple answer to the nature of infesting evil, regardless of our interpretations, will suffice. Man has wrestled with evil on this earth across untold ages.

Baptist minister Walter R. Martin, pastor of the Van Riper Memorial Church in Fair Lawn, New Jersey, director of the

---

2 Dietrich Bonhoeffer, *Ethics,* translated by Neville Horton Smith. New York: The Macmillan Co., 1965, p. 245.

Christian Research Institute in Wayne, New Jersey, and author of many works on religion, told this writer: "When Jesus was tempted in the wilderness, the tempter had to be outside of Jesus, not within Him. For Jesus, the Son of God, knows that it is God's world. How could the tempter offer Jesus what was already His because it was God's? Therefore Christians must accept the converse—that the temptations came to Jesus from an *outside* entity. And this entity could only be defined as Satan."

Martin is convinced, with many millions of his coreligionists, that we must accept the idea of a devil who preys upon us and seeks to destroy us. On the issue of possession, he told me, "I know a psychiatrist, one of the best known in New York, a practicing Christian, who has had a number of cases in which he was convinced that he was dealing not with a mere psychological disorder within the individual but with an entity that had to be removed by some form of exorcism."

The varieties of belief in demonology remain many and diverse.

A Layman's Guide to Baptist Beliefs by the Rev. Harold L. Fickett, Jr., asserts a fundamental belief in the final defeat of Satan at Armageddon as described in the Book of Revelation. The points are spelled out with precision and exactitude:

"A. *The Lord Jesus Christ is going to return to this earth* followed by a celestial army made up of the saints of all ages. His twofold purpose in coming will be that of judging and making war (Revelation 19:11–14).

"B. Blood will play a prominent part in His Second Coming as it did in His first coming. We are told that He will be clothed in a vesture dipped in blood (Revelation 19:13). Unlike His first coming where His shed blood was the means of atonement, the vesture dipped in blood will be a sign of bloody judgment upon His adversaries (Isaiah 63:2–3). . . .

"C. *In His return He will not come as the "Suffering Servant"* as He did in His first coming; instead He will come manifesting

Himself as the King of Kings and Lord of Lords (Revelation 19:15–16). As such He will be ready to fulfill. (Isaiah 9:6–7).

"D. *His coming will precipitate the Battle of Armageddon* which will eventuate in the destruction of His enemies. . . .

"E. *The devil will be taken out of the world* and chained for one thousand years (Revelation 20:1–3).

"F. During the time that the devil is restricted *Christ will reign as the world's benevolent dictator.* He will be seated on David's throne in the city of Jerusalem . . ."[3]

Despite a lack of widespread publicity in recent years, Satan manages to hold his position in the formalities of modern faith. In the Roman Catholic faith, when adults are baptized, they ritually declare in response to the priest:

"P: Do you renounce Satan?

"ALL: I do renounce him.

"P: And all his works?

"ALL: I do renounce them.

"P: And all his attractions?

"ALL: I do renounce them."[4]

And in the Episcopal baptism of adults:

"Question: Dost thou renounce the devil and all his works, the vain pomp and glory of the world, with all covetous desires of the same, and the sinful desires of the flesh, so that thou wilt not follow, nor be led by them?

"*Answer:* I renounce them all; and, by God's help, will endeavor not to follow, nor be led by them."[5]

The history of the demons and drumbeats is long, bewildering, frightening. Most of the peoples of the world are theologically confused; belief in a literal heaven and hell waits on the latest

---

[3] Harold L. Fickett, Jr., *A Layman's Guide to Baptist Beliefs.* Grand Rapids, Michigan: Zondervan Publishing House, 1965, pp. 176–7.

[4] Phillip T. Weller, S.T.D. *The Roman Ritual.* Milwaukee: The Bruce Publishing Co., 1964, p. 85.

[5] *The Book of Common Prayer.* New York: Oxford University Press, 1898, p. 261.

signals from rockets in outer space. Religious absolutes are fragmented against hard realities.

How primitive our concepts of the devil seem against the choices of good and evil we ourselves hold in our frightened hands! Yet these demons of the past die hard. The folklore lives; the stories, the legends, blend into half-truth and old wives' tales.

Writers of Catholic books in the past provided detailed accounts of the works of the devil in action. Yet many Roman Catholics—including some priests—have expressed to this writer opinions that clearly indicate they do not believe in a personal demon. The literal concept of the devil is not, in fact, accepted universally in any of the major denominations.

A Roman Catholic priest, Father John L. Thomas, S.J., directed a very carefully conducted survey, the techniques and questions of which were examined and approved by Dr. George Gallup as free from bias in orientation or wording. The actual testing was carried out by a Chicago marketing and research company, Ben Gaffin and Associates. The questionnaire attempted to cover an objective cross section of adult Americans of all faiths—including those with no religious preference or who profess to belong to some religion but never go to church. The survey revealed that 77 percent of the respondents believed the soul survived human death (meaning that more than 20 percent did *not* believe in survival as preached in the traditional faiths). A somewhat smaller number—72 percent—affirmed that they believed in Heaven. Interestingly, however, only 58 percent asserted that they believed in Hell. Although Roman Catholics ranked higher in affirmation of questions involving traditional faith, it is interesting to note that only 74 percent of them affirmed a belief in Hell.

Father Thomas, in discussing this in his book *Religion and the American People,* declares, "It is easy to miss the profound implications of these findings because the term *Hell* has come to be regarded as nothing more than a byword in vulgar speech.

Considered in the perspective of Christian realism, however, Hell is the alternative to justification and salvation. The essential human dilemma as viewed by the Christian is man separated from God by sin—fallen man in need of redemption through Christ. The alternative is Hell. . . . To deny the existence of Hell is implicitly to deny the need for redemption. In the traditional Christian definition of the situation, to redeem implies a freeing from sin, and consequently from eternal alienation in Hell, as well as a freeing for divine friendship and its culmination in Heaven. . . . Viewed in the light of these considerations, the fact that over one out of every four Roman Catholics and almost half of the Protestants no longer believe in the existence of Hell may be judged highly significant."[6]

Although no question was asked directly as to the reality of Satanic forces, it is logical to assume that belief in Satan might be divided in the same proportions recorded by those who did or did not believe in the reality of Hell.

Whatever division exists, the more enlightened modern clergymen have moved away from a demon-oriented religion. In a statement to this writer, Dr. Norman Vincent Peale summed up much of the modern view:

"Throughout the ministry of Jesus, we find that He puts the greater emphasis on the affirmative message of God's love for us, of the Kingdom that is within us if we learn to recognize it, of the love that we must have for God, His world, His people.

"These are the affirmations. He is telling us of a world that's good to live in, and of a life that brings good to all. When he speaks of Satan, he speaks of him as the opposite force of evil in the world to which the good is in opposition. Of himself and his own missions, he says, 'I am the Way, the Truth and the Life.' And again, 'I am the Light of the world,' as contrasted with its darkness.

---

[6] John L. Thomas, S.J., *Religion and the American People*. Westminster, Maryland: The Newman Press, 1963, pp. 60–61.

"It seems to me that the Christian has enough to do already following that road of Light and Life He shows us, to concern himself too much about the darkness and what devils may dwell within it. Those who dwell in Christian love do not need to concern themselves with such terrors and demons."

CHAPTER XI

GHOSTS, MEN, AND GOD

Spiritism differs from spiritualism in that the former is concerned only with spirits and what they do, whereas spiritualism is in itself a religion and as such has been denounced often as a cult. Spiritualists insist even more firmly than other faiths that they have the truth, for they believe not only in survival of the personality but also in the ability of these personalities to communicate with the living.

Organized religion, including fundamentalist faiths and Roman Catholicism, has long been opposed to all such beliefs, partly because of the danger of fraud, and partly because of fear of demonic involvements. Yet individuals in these faiths do delve into the supernatural. And individual priests, for example, do publish learned papers and reports on spiritualistic encounters that would be hard to divorce from the spiritism of the spiritualist movement itself.

Theologically, the church for centuries has placed its comfort and faith in the resurrection of Christ, in his triumph over death and his promise of eternal life to all who follow his way.

Most modern theologians do not try to spell out what the afterworld will be like except in the most general terms. But some go into considerable detail concerning heaven, hell, and limbo.

It is not illogical that spiritualism should abound with varied descriptions of the world beyond as believers envision or interpret it. They claim to hear the voices or see the individuals in their descriptions of "the other side."

But since Christianity does preach survival as a part of its faith—is there an essential clash between Christian and spiritualistic concepts?

One of the sharpest statements on the chasm between Christianity and spiritualism appears in *The Challenge of the Sects,* a book issued by the Westminster Press, the publishing arm of the Presbyterian Church. Written by Horton Davies, professor of the history of Christianity at Princeton University, the book describes the basic divergences in essence as follows:

1. Christianity puts its basic reliance on the teachings of Jesus Christ and on God's "might" of raising Jesus from the dead. The spiritualists—"spiritists," as Davies calls them—claim that their information on survival after death and the nature of the afterlife is received from the dead themselves.

2. Christianity defines immortality, says Davies, as a gift of God bestowed on those who have merited salvation; the spiritists claim that the afterlife is "automatic"—that it belongs to all people regardless of the grace of God.

3. According to Davies, the spiritist's picture of the afterlife is "spiritually superficial and tawdry," whereas in the Christian view the afterlife is not merely "an automatic rest cure" but is primarily "the blessedness of everlasting fellowship with God and His saints."[1]

Obviously, Professor Davies is not speaking for all Christians

---

[1] Horton Davies, *The Challenge of the Sects.* Philadelphia: The Westminster Press, 1961, p. 63.

in this critique, but there can be little doubt that he reflects attitudes with which most major Christian denominations concur.

Few religions that oppose spiritualism and its practices, however, take any stand against the possibility or the reality of spiritualistic phenomena. The basic assault is on theological, Christian grounds and on the fear of involvement with dangerous forces.

In contrast, Dr. J. B. Rhine, the parapsychologist, takes an entirely opposite track. He is clearly on record, both in his statements and writings and in his actions, that religion is in error when it does not support investigations into the nature of the "psi" in whatever psychic way "psi" expresses itself. Throughout his writings he insists that we put aside old notions if they are proved untrue.

"If . . . some kind of world of independent spirit agency can be discovered, as there is reason to believe possible, its establishment would manifestly bring to religious life an incomparably greater meaning and potency. The discovery would do for religion something like what the germ theory did for medicine. It would open the range of religious exploration to horizons beyond all present conceptions. . . ."[2]

Religion finds itself here, as in so much of today's paranormal activity, facing uninhibited questions that some church leaders would prefer to ignore. The young intellectuals of the church want a Bonhoeffer-oriented evangelism dedicated to this world and its needs. Other churchmen basically prefer a religion centered on the individual loving God and opposing sin, and the Devil, in any possible shape or form.

Yet others, in the church and out, insist that there is no part of this world or any other that does not concern God and Christ— and that therefore should not concern all the rest of us as well.

In his writings, Dr. Rhine has urged that we should investigate

---

[2] J. B. Rhine, *New World of the Mind.* New York: William Sloane Associates, 1953, p. 238.

all psychic effects, discarding the false, cleaning away the dregs so that, as he puts it, we can examine, in complete scientific objectivity and thoroughness, whatever remains.

But there is no question that religion has serious reservations in the ancient but now scientifically revived area of spirit phenomena.

Bluntly stated, the fear of fakery has become one of the greatest problems in the spiritualistic field in the United States today. Mediumship in the United States does not receive the respect it enjoys in, say, the United Kingdom. The great peril in the eyes of many ministers and priests is that the individual seeking spiritualistic experience may become involved with forces he does not understand and is not equipped to handle.

Consider one brochure advertising a book by a well-known psychic authority, which promises a tremendous potential: "NOW! Call upon these mighty Beings from the 'Invisible World' around you—and INSTANTLY begin a wonderful new life of wealth, love and happiness! . . . These creatures can be put to many uses. They can guard your house, protect your family, carry messages for you, let you know what others say about you behind your back, help you find lost objects—even make you rich! You'll find full details on Pages 155–170 . . ."[3]

The brochure goes on to name some of these "invisible be-ings" as "poltergeists," "elementals," "the little people," and "the Group Mind otherwise called the Collective Mass Mind," and to promise from them:

"Endless streams of money, gold, silver and jewels.

"Radiant, glowing health and boundless strength and energy.

"The irresistible sex appeal of a movie star.

"Amazing psychic powers, such as telepathy, levitation, etc.

"Control over others, and the ability to dominate anyone you meet instantly.

[3] Mail-order advertisement for book entitled *Between Two Worlds* by Nandor Foder.

"Tremendous wisdom and peace of mind, profound spiritual treasures . . ."[4]

Such copy hardly needs comment. But it is part of the picture.

The issue resolves itself to this: Can modern religion afford to ignore or oppose investigations of psychic matters today, any more than it can oppose investigation of government, social issues, race issues, psychology and psychiatry, sex education for the young, or vaccination against disease?

Whatever the answer, many if not most of the modern churches still oppose spiritualistic teachings and practice with all the weight of their authority.

Declares Seventh Day Adventist Ellen G. White in *The Great Controversy:*

"Many will be confronted by the spirits of devils personating beloved relatives or friends and declaring the most dangerous heresies. These visitants will appeal to our tenderest sympathies and will work miracles to sustain their pretensions. We must be prepared to withstand them with the Bible truth that the dead know not anything and that they who thus appear are the spirits of devils."[5]

It would appear that many religions oppose spiritualism on three grounds: the possibility of fraudulent mediums; the possibility of demonic deception; and the possibility of psychopathic or neurotic self-deception on the part of the individual.

The noted British clergyman and religious authority Leslie Weatherhead cites a case in which a spirit doctor, speaking "through" a medium, advised a woman against an appendectomy that her surgeon had said was urgently required. Fortunately, the pain did not disappear as the spiritualist had predicted it would. The woman returned to the physician and had the operation, and her life was saved.

---

[4] *Ibid.*

[5] Ellen G. White, *The Great Controversy.* Mountain View, California: Pacific Press Publishing Association, 1950, p. 560.

Yet Weatherhead, elsewhere in his famous work *Psychology, Religion and Healing,* insists that the spiritualistic approach— under strict controls that do not violate proper medical practices or guidance—should at least be investigated carefully.

Baptist pastor Walter Martin, in his study of the cults, however, cites three major reasons for denouncing what he calls the "Cult of Spiritualism": that in order to embrace its teachings, one must renounce every major doctrine of Christianity; that supernaturalistic manifestations in spiritualism originate, according to the Bible, in demonic forces and are therefore under the judgment of God; and that Christians must realize that spiritists "wilfully ignore" the God of the Bible and the meaning of God's sending His Son to save the world.

"In the spirit of Christian love, we are committed to bear witness against the Spiritists, refute their teachings, and confront them with the Christ of Calvary . . ."[6]

But it is clear that many in the churches believe they have a right to probe and to know—not in the mystic beyond, but in the present world—the answer, the glimpse behind the curtain.

---

[6] Walter R. Martin, *The Kingdom of the Cults,* Grand Rapids, Michigan: Zondervan Publishing House, 1965, p. 212.

CHAPTER XII

WE THE POSSESSED

"I adjure you, ancient serpent," the Catholic priest declares, "by the judge of the living and the dead, by your Creator, by the Creator of the whole universe, by Him who has the power to consign you to hell, to depart forthwith in fear, along with your savage minions, from this servant of God . . ."[1]

So the priest intones the words of the Roman Ritual, the official Roman Catholic rites of exorcism prescribed for those possessed by demons or other entities.

The belief in actual physical possession is deeply imbedded in human and religious history. Churches that believe in devils and other discarnate entities also accept the idea that such demons try to act through men and women and children and can infest houses and people.

Belief in possession by spirits runs back to the paleolithic beginnings of civilization and is found in all later cultures. The savage in the jungle, when someone is ill or out of his mind with

---

[1] Philip Weller, S.T.D., *The Roman Ritual.* Milwaukee: The Bruce Publishing Co., 1964, p. 651.

fever, prays for the evil spirit to depart and entreats the good deities to drive out the bad. Belief in such notions is found in all parts of the world. The writer knows of a case in Brazil in which a witch doctor was about to put to death a ten-year-old child on the ground that she was possessed of a demon. A Christian missionary rescued her and escaped with her in a small boat, with the witch doctor and his adherents pursuing in canoes. They reached the safety of the mission house some miles down the river before the natives could overtake them.

Yet Christianity has also had a long history of faith in demonic possession, as have other religions. For example, in Biblical times, it was accepted almost without question that those who acted strangely were possessed. When Jesus healed the boy with the falling-down illness, the gospel reports that Jesus drove the demons out of the boy and told his disciples afterward that this kind of demon goes out only with much fasting and prayer.

Was Jesus speaking, as many modern theologians today believe, only in the terminology of his times, without meaning his words literally, or did he actually mean that there were beings, entities, coexisting in the body of the boy?

Throughout the Middle Ages, theories and detailed analyses of how devils possess and what they make people do were developed to a point at which exorcism became a high ritualistic art and the sadomasochistic tendencies of some exorcists found a religiously acceptable outlet. Virtually all the mentally ill were considered possessed of demons by the God-fearing, average citizens of that day. Luther and Calvin concurred completely in such ideas.

Volumes could be filled detailing the stories of alleged possession in Europe and in America from the fifteenth century to the dawn of the twentieth. The Salem hysteria in which children claimed they were possessed by demons through the agency of witches whom they accused—and damned to death—was only one unusually sensational example of generally accepted demon-theology. This was fully supported and spread by many leading theologians of the time, particularly, in America, by the famous peacher Cotton Mather. The credibility gap that began to develop in this case, and ultimately led to its being demolished as an openly admitted fraud, was one of the first great blows against the witchcraft-demonology syndrome of that age.

As the age of reason progressed into the age of science and a new incandescence began to light the dark corners, demons were no longer in style, religiously or among the laity. In the twentieth century the more enlightened elements in the churches began to talk less and less about demons and to substitute, where indicated, the term "demonic." The demon in large measure ceased to be an entity, a being with a voice of its own; it became merely a demonic force, a depersonalized abstraction, a thing called evil.

It is not surprising that the modern church should hesitate to discuss officially the issue of possession. For this is surely one of the most bleak, and in some cases most brutal, segments of organized religion, both Catholic and Protestant. The record of the mentally ill who were treated as possessed, with vicious sadistic beatings to drive out the "demon," and the record of so-called witches and their "confessions" so patently forced by punishment and torture, is a sorry one from which religion has been long recovering.

"One Foster, who confessed her own share in the Witchcraft for which the Prisoner stood indicted affirm'd, that she had seen the prisoner at some of their Witch-meetings. . . . She confessed that the Devil carry'd them on a pole, to a Witch-meeting . . ."[2]

The term Sabbat was employed to describe these meetings of witches at which the devil presided. The witches were said to fly up their chimneys and across the sky to attend the Sabbats, which took place at midnight, with all their orgiastic activities

---

[2] Montague Summers, *The History of Witchcraft*, New Hyde Park, New York, University Books, 1956, p. 124.

celebrating what was called "the witches' Sabbath." Torture, fear, superstition, and hysteria produced often lengthy confessions detailing the events of the Sabbat—how the devil climbed into the pulpit of the church and made every witch present kiss his exposed buttocks and perform other obscenities too vile to put into print.

Whipping the devil out of the possessed sometimes resulted in death. The phrase "to whip the devil" out of someone is another living remnant of this religious sadism.

Most unbelievable is the length of time it took—in centuries —for ecclesiastical officialdom to begin to understand its own diagnostic errors.

Even doctors were reluctant to challenge accepted religious views. The "snake pit" for the insane fed on the heartless laughter of onlookers peering through the bars. That it is still with us today, in some institutions, can no longer be placed at the doorstep of religion. But that some of the earlier ideas survive, that some of the more superstitious prelates and ministers still cringe before the devil in the shadows, is still a fact.

Is there true possession in the literal sense of an entity taking over an individual?

Dr. H. Peter Laqueur, noted American psychiatrist and supervising psychiatrist at Creedmore State Hospital in New York, declares that possession is a peril "as an idea in the mind of the supposedly possessed." Dr. Laqueur may have restored more psychotics to normal life than any other physician in the world. Schizophrenics of all types have been restored to permanent normal living by his use of chemo-psychotherapeutic techniques.

Laqueur's whole approach is to bring the patient as quickly as possible to a state of cooperation and calm.

"If someone thinks he is possessed," Dr. Laqueur told me, "for him the possession is real. He believes the devil is in him, making him do this or that terrible thing. How do we help him to get over this? The simplest and best method, I have found, is to bring in a priest or minister to confer with him, to listen to his story and to assure him that he does not have a demon. He may not believe the priest, but he can be helped by the priest to see that even if he did have a demon as he believes, the demon could not control him or make him do evil. All he has to do is to say no to these inner urgings. Thus he begins to get insight that this demon within him has no ability to harm him, that in fact it has no reality unless he lets it have reality."

This is, in a sense, a form of exorcism. The reassurance of pastor or priest that the person is not possessed, or that prayers and other religious acts have aided in making this devil harmless, enables him to accept the idea that he must permit the doctors to help him get rid of his delusions and restore him to reality.

Dr. Laqueur declares: "Once the patient who believes himself driven by a demon knows that there is no demon within him, or at any rate knows that no demon within him can do him harm— that the demonic force has been neutralized—the true psychotherapy can begin. We have been working with new techniques in insulin and other drugs combined with psychotherapy, occupational therapy, family therapy, where we work with all those involved in an immediate family, and group family therapy, where we work with several families of the mentally ill at once."

Often, Dr. Laqueur reports, close relatives of the supposedly "demon possessed" are unaware of the part they may have played in the "possession." Nor do they know the role they can and must play—in care, in understanding, in concern—to help him stay whole after his release.

In May, 1966, Father Matthew Peiris, an Anglican priest who is a native of Ceylon, India, came to America and began to preach and practice exorcism in Houston, Texas. As of this writing, it is reported that he has driven demons out of some twenty-five possessed persons.

Father Peiris maintains that the demons are real and that they are dangerous. "They are evil personalities," he declared in an interview, "living in a spirit world of their own, occasionally dominating, intruding, attacking and controlling men, women and children."[3]

The number of persons he has exorcised, including those in the United States, is more than two hundred.

One way in which he describes such possessed people is that they seem to be beyond space and time; they seem to know things that may be happening miles away; they seem to be able to cross the dimensions of space and time, to places and events out of the past that they could not have known by any normal means.

In his exorcisms Father Peiris used the simple vestments of the church and the two candles on the altar. As a priest, he believes in God, of course; but he also believes that God has a spirited enemy "in the person of the prince of darkness, which is Satan, demons, evil personalities."[4]

Over the centuries, the field in which possession was a possible explanation for a person's behavior has shrunk inexorably, as the knowledge and understanding of mental sickness has progressed. Well, some ask, was there possession by demons in the time of Jesus that no longer happens today? Did the demons really leave the demented man and enter pigs, which thereupon plunged into the sea? Or was Jesus merely reflecting the understanding of his time, the human Jesus speaking as a human, but the divine Jesus speaking and acting at a higher level, to heal men who were essentially the mentally ill of that day?

In connection with the Biblical account, Leslie Weatherhead raises an interesting speculation: When the demented man, in response to Jesus, replies that his name is Legion, could he have been referring not to demons but to a memory, to a shock of childhood, when the Roman Legion, known for its cruelty and murder of women and children, was cutting a bloodletting path

---

[3] Houston *Post*, Houston, Texas, Aug. 14, 1966.
[4] *Ibid.*

across the countryside? Did he as a child see a massacre of children in the streets red with blood, and run to his home crying out, as Weatherhead reshapes it in modern terms, "Mummy, mummy—Legion." And later in new traumatic moments echo these words: "Our name is Legion."

There is no doubt that Jesus healed the man according to Mark's gospel report. The question is rather whether Mark's interpretation and Weatherhead's suggestions are correct—according to modern psychological thinking.

The episode could be explained quite literally—even to the panic-prone swine hurling themselves over the cliff at the cries of the herdsmen and the unusual excitement. But these are beguiling theories only, which modern man—and his church—begin to examine and reexamine in modern terms.

There are those who believe in possession. There are others who believe themselves to be possessed and who go for help to the clergyman as often as to the doctor or psychiatrist. There are also tens of thousands who believe in spiritualism, in which entities "possess" the medium in the role of "guides." Many of the seriously mentally ill insist that beings possess them and make them commit vile acts and crimes.

There are, in addition, cases in psychiatry involving true "split personalities" of the Jekyll-Hyde type. Most noted is the case detailed in the book and motion picture "The Three Faces of Eve," in which a psychiatrist reports the true story of a patient who had three distinct personalities within her being. One personality would dominate for a time and then, usually without warning or seeming reason, another would move in, whereupon the woman's voice, expression, language, and attitude would instantly change.

The first personality—Eve White—had a normal outlook, but rejected herself. The second—Eve Black—had a more turbulent outlook, a self-satisfaction through which she appeared to achieve "a violent kind of adjustment in which she perceives

herself as literally perfect. . . ." Jane, the third personality in
Eve, appeared better adjusted than either of the other two, to the
world and to herself.

Both Eve Black and Jane were shadow personalities that had
taken over within Eve White. Psychotherapy over many months
freed the girl from these secondary personalities and all the
dangers they presented. But the question of how these other personalities were formed within her, and why, remains unanswered
by psychiatry. Were they outside entities that took possession?
Or misformed psychological fragments of the same personality?

One might find many answers, but none would be conclusive.
What is conclusive is that despite the church's new modernism
and social outlook, possession remains as a seeming reality in its
midst. Whatever shape or interpretation we give it, the idea will
not die easily. It was as strong in the modern metropolis of
Houston, Texas, as in the shadowed jungles of Ceylon.

A distinguished French neurologist, Dr. Jean Lhermitte,
member of the French Académie Nationale de Médicin, states,
in the closing paragraphs of his book on *True and False Possession,* that there are cases of both real and false possession and
that they must be carefully distinguished. His point is, in a sense,
a double-edged knife in psychiatry's back:

"One last question for the theorist: When the devil enters into
a man's soul and body, can he reveal his presence exclusively by
the semblance of a mental or bodily illness? In other words,
when the doctor recognizes in a patient all the elements of a
definite disease, has he the right to see in it *only* the effects of a
natural process, even when a scientific treatment is able to cure
it?"[5]

Having raised his sharply pointed query, Dr. Lhermitte then
turns and runs. His next and final paragraph declares: "It is not

---

[5] Jean Lhermitte, *True and False Possession,* translated from the French by
P. J. Hepburne-Scott. New York: Hawthorn Books, 1963, p. 125.

for me to resolve this problem, and on this point the reader must form his own judgment according to his beliefs."[6]

This is the unanswered question.

It is possible that the church will face the issue in a new way, under new circumstances and on new grounds. For while demonic possession still is an accepted reality by many religions, a new kind of possession has begun to take shape in the modern world—possession by drugs, possession brought on not by demons but by a few drops of "acid" that take over the individual.

Mind-expanding drugs, delusion-creating drugs, create a distortion of reality by which the individual is possessed, changed, controlled, often destroyed, with all the virulent irrationality of ancient demon-haunted superstition.

Are the chemicals of the new drugs comparable to the demons of old beliefs? Can they provide a truly mystical or religious experience, as some users claim they do? Or do they merely take possession?

---

[6] *Ibid.*, p. 125.

DRUMS AND DREAMS

In the 1960's the way-out groups, including some religious leaders, suggested that men must explore the Kingdom of God that
Jesus speaks of not only by the avenues of religion or psychology
but also over the new trails opened to us by use of mind-changing drugs.

The following report was published in *The New York Times*
on June 26, 1966:

"There is a widespread view, particularly among young people, that marijuana and LSD (lysergic acid diethylamide) are no
more harmful than the alcohol in a cocktail or the nicotine in a
cigarette. They consider those who seek to control their use as
'old maids.'

"What, in fact, is the view of the medical community? In a
recent Bulletin of the World Health Organization four well-
known pharmacologists said that marijuana (known interna-
tionally as cannabis) can lead to 'lethargy, self-neglect, feeling of
increased capability, with corresponding failure, and precipita-
tion of psychotic episodes.' It can encourage contacts with those

using more dangerous drugs, such as opiates or barbiturates, inducing the victim to shift to such truly addictive drugs.

"LSD can produce either euphoria or deep depression, the group said. It is thus an occasional cause of suicide. It has also been reported that, at least in excessive doses, it permanently alters the chemistry of the brain. This may explain the claims of those who, after treatment with LSD, report a long-lasting change in their outlook on life.

"The W.H.O. report was prepared by Dr. Nathan B. Eddy of the National Institutes of Health in Bethesda, Maryland. Dr. Hans Halbach of W.H.O.; Dr. Harris Isbell of the University of Kentucky; and Dr. Maurice H. Seevers of the University of Michigan."

Another report told of a woman in a Western state, who, while under the influence of LSD, became excessively depressed and killed her baby. She cut out its heart and replaced it with a whiskey bottle. When authorities arrested her they noted she was in a severe trance.

This writer has talked to a number of clergymen who have experimented in these new fields. Some had only one or two "trips," others apparently many more.

One of the clergymen interviewed, pastor of a large and wealthy church in New York City, described his experience with LSD in the following statement, written from notes after my return from an evening in consultation with him:

"I prepared for this experience carefully. I felt that it was something I should undergo, something I should know. Everything was set up properly, carefully. To assist me, as I set forth on this 'trip' a record player played music—a piano concerto by Beethoven, one I particularly love, Beethoven's Fourth. The music to me has always provided a tremendous exhilaration. This time, I was not transported as usual into a dream world. It was exactly the reverse. It was as if the dream world were the one in which I lived usually and this other world into which I walked were the reality.

"This is an extremely difficult thing to describe because it involves a totality of dream and reality merged, the totality of self and other selves, of awareness that senses, accepts, knows without knowing to an extent far beyond anything I had ever before grasped or suspected as being possible in one mind, one human mind.

"As you listen you suddenly see the horizon of the world, the overpowering beauty, without evil. Evil dies and there is only the good; you know where you are and still you know this other new intensity. It is like a vehicle rolling over air, rolling through the air. There is a total sensory apprehension. Houses, buildings, people, trains, experiences that were both real and unreal, actual and fantasy. But to me there was no fantasy. I felt that the universe and I were one; and I could never be alone, I could never be alone again, in life or death. It is a deeply moving experience which I consider to be of an essentially religious character because it makes life closer, more understandable. It makes God closer to me . . ."

I do not know if this minister tried the experiment again. I do know him to be a respected and popular minister, conservative in most aspects of his religious activities.

Others I have talked with described episodes of varying characteristics—but all intensifying not only the world but also the religious element. There is a reluctance by most ministers who have tried the drug to allow their names to be used publicly in connection with it. They are eager for the experience on the one hand—and fearful that their parishioners would seek their removal if the episodes became public information.

One who has *not* experimented with such things is Dr. Erwin Seale of the Church of the Truth in New York, one of the important workers in metaphysical healing. Dr. Seale centers his faith and teachings in the reality of Christ in our lives today, in all who seek to know Him. Can this be done by a drug? Dr. Seale questions such a bizarre approach.

Pointing to its potential dangers, he declares, "I had a friend who tried it and who during its period of effect studied a rose. For more than one hour he studied the rose with all the intensity of awareness that is reported in these LSD experiences; the rose and he were one thing, the rose and he were the universe. I am anything but convinced that this kind of episode has any significant role in religion.

"The unpredictable reactions of those who take this drug have little to do with the kind of orthodox Christian experience produced by truly religious experience."

Yet it is in the garb of a new religion that LSD is presented, with much fanfare and publicity.

LSD "religion" began to take shape when its most publicized "prophet," Dr. Timothy Leary, after being discharged from the Harvard faculty for his activities with LSD, set up his temple to LSD in a former movie house on Second Avenue, New York. What began as a sincere attempt to explore the psychic qualities of a drug became what one drama expert in New York was caustic enough to describe as no more than plain "show biz." Declared critic John Gruen with regard to the garish performance, complete with bare feet, beatniks and tourists, microphones, psychedelic movies, voice sound tracks and paying audience: "Religion as Show Biz is making it big on Second Avenue. Dr. Timothy Leary's LSD rites at the Village Theatre have already become a Tuesday evening staple of the East Village."[1]

The sibilant syllables of Dr. Leary echo in the shadows: "It's always the Last Supper when you take the sacraments." But by sacraments he refers not to the communion of wine and bread—but to LSD.

Drugs of various types have long been employed to probe the fortress of consciousness. The "mind-changing" drugs, the hallucinogenics, come in various forms, under a host of names. The numerous variations of hemp, for example, both cultivated and

---

[1] John Gruen, "The Pop Scene." *World Journal Tribune,* Nov. 22, 1966, p. 31.

wild, are found in all parts of the world under perhaps half a hundred or more names. In the course of writing two books on narcotics, the author investigated—not by personal use but by first-hand interviews and personal reports of users—the effects of many of these drugs and the changes in sensory apperception: a room becomes suddenly larger, "growing" from a dingy downtown "pad" to a vast hollow hall of dream-like impact; the voices of people standing close by seem far off; and it seems to take five minutes to walk a distance of only twenty feet or less.

In Greece, my wife and I once visited the ruins of the greatest oracle of antiquity—Delphi, the holy of holies in ancient Greece, with great white crags rising above it and, far below, the sea of olive trees once owned by the ancient priesthood of the shrine. Here the Sibyls in the midst of the fumes of the gods made their sacred pronouncements, ancestral voices prophesying war and peace, victory and disaster.

Some historians believe the Delphic fumes were produced by one of the cannabis drugs—the hemp weed which has so many aliases around the world. *Cannabis sativa americana* is the scientific name of the plant that produces marijuana, a variety of the drug popularly called hashish. Hashish gave its name to an early band of religionists—the Assassins—who used the drug. The dictionary says the word comes from *hashshashin,* meaning hashish-eaters. It is also said that hashish was named for an Eastern religio-warlord named Hasan whose followers devoted themselves to ridding the Moslem world of false prophets of Mohammed.

For thousands of years, the use of drugs has been associated with alleged religious experience. How often drugs may have been responsible for the "visions" that pervade all religions, especially in the Orient, is a matter of conjecture.

It is known that the Aztecs used peyote, a rather insignificant member of the cactus family on the basis of size or appearance, but which within its roots holds fire and excitement, to some a heavenly and to others perhaps a hellish meaning. In recent years Aldous Huxley wrote warmly and beautifully of its power and glory—as though it were a god. Natives of Central America are said to venerate it because it provides release and beauty and meaning in a world, they say, that has no direction. Centuries ago, the Aztecs also had a mushroom they considered sacred because it had similar powers. They called it *teonancatl,* which has been translated as meaning "the flesh of God."

Peyote is found in the peyotl button (called "button" because of the greenish-gray top part of the plant) and it contains the image-inducing alkaloid, mescaline. This, in combination with other alkaloids in the plant, produces unusual sense-changing reactions. In seventeenth-century Spanish America, Catholic authorities denounced the peyotl cactus as a product of the Evil One and banned its use by natives or others.

However, use of the peyotl buttons, otherwise misnamed mescal buttons, continued to some extent, secretly and even openly. By the middle of the nineteenth century, use of the drug in the southwestern part of the United States and in Mexico was soaring. By 1875, a whole new "peyotl religion" was under way. By the middle of the twentieth century, there were estimated to be perhaps three to four hundred thousand peyotl users, among the tribes of the Southwest and in a spreading "peyotl religion" among white people, particularly those influenced by the descriptions of release and intensification of consciousness by writers such as Aldous Huxley and Havelock Ellis.

Two aspects of hallucinogenic drugs, old or new, grown or manufactured, are often overlooked by the defenders of their use: Whether or not they are harmful physically, and whether or not the so-called religious experiences are true religious experiences.

The four pharmacologists who reported to the World Health Organization on narcotics and their effects declared that there is no evidence that marijuana permanently damages the central nervous system or builds a tolerance that requires an increasing dosage. It has been established, however, that this drug, like cigarettes or coffee, is habit-forming and often does lead to increased usage—or more dangerously becomes a stepping-stone to the "killer drug" heroin.

Religiously, or otherwise, LSD has even more penetrating and profound effects. It is a volatile force. No one knows the sum total of results. There have been medical reports of serious injury, the possibility of permanent psychological dislocation and brain damage. LSD reactions have occurred in patients months after use of the drug, in the form of severe anxiety, depression, and confusion of which they could not free themselves.

Physicians involved in this research reported in the *Journal* of the American Medical Association that their findings pointed to a real danger in the increasing number of disabilities resulting from LSD reactions.

A book entitled *The Varieties of Psychedelic Experience,* by R. E. L. Masters and Jean Houston, quotes a description of a religio-psychic experience in the very depths of the LSD trip:

"Whenever I looked at myself in the mirror during the other sessions I was always surrounded by darkness. But now I am surrounded by light. I saw myself in the mirror before as looking like the Devil. My image in the mirror was each time that of the Devil. And I have seen it often before in my life, without any drugs. As of several years ago I started seeing this Devil image in the mirror less often. But now I see my own face surrounded by light and somehow the face is changed in other ways I can't yet describe. This seems to me to be some kind of defeat for the Devil and at the same time I feel a hope with regard to myself that I never felt before. The hope seems to be a kind of awareness of the possibility of my being delivered from all punishments I feel I've had to bear for what I never did . . . as if I were the one who had to bear the burden of the Devil into the world as a little child and then had to live with it."[2]

Individual ministers play whatever role seems best, but the major churches are leaving investigation and participation to others. To the evangelical faiths these drugs remain manifestations of the devil except when medically used. All major religions actively oppose uncontrolled use of any narcotics or drugs of a dangerous nature. Many churches, particularly among the Episcopalians, have priests and ministers assigned to conduct missions to help the victims of drug traffic, particularly the victims of heroin and marijuana. This writer has taught Sunday School classes in narcotics-ridden metropolitan districts where every tenement on the block, and virtually every child in the church school, had had some experience with narcotics and drug pushers.

The Urban Training Center for Christian Mission in Chicago, a training place for young ministers and laymen, provides a startling contrast in true religious experience. Instead of meeting a chemically coated world of intensified illusions, those who attend the Center go out into the actual world to meet the reality of people in need; theirs is an internship in humanity, without funds, friends, influence. Here they meet the drug users. During their penniless days in the streets, the "interns" actually live the life of the unemployed, mingling in their world, going through all the real experiences that these people undergo in Chicago.

A report on this kind of religious experience and reality provides far different answers from those found in the LSD hallucinatory journeys.

---

[2] R. E. L. Masters and Jean Houston, *The Varieties of Psychedelic Experience*. New York, Chicago, San Francisco: Holt, Rinehart and Winston, 1966, p. 290.

CHAPTER XIV

WITHIN THE WALLS

St. Robert's Roman Catholic Church in Chittenden, Vermont, should be a rustic edifice, in the white-clapboard tradition of all New England churches. It is, in fact, of ultra-modern design. Vermonters, summer visitors and residents, come here to worship in the modern pews, in the hush of the simple but definitely "different" interior.

Vermont Catholics—like all Vermonters—cling to the past and shy away from the new. Yet one woman who worshiped in this modernistic country church told me: "We like the new designs, the new altar, the new way of worship in English, the new way the priest faces us. All of it makes more sense; it makes us a part of what is happening."

Churches were built in eras before electric lights, air-cooling systems, steel structures. The church edifice became the refuge in war, in actual battle, against the arrows of the enemy.

But now the houses of God, as built by men, have changed as much as the rituals and liturgy by which we worship. Startling and often controversial changes in church architecture have un-

123

folded in the decades since World War II. Not only the outside of the buildings but the inside structural design, lighting, and form have undergone radical alteration.

In Europe, religion was the ancient Gothic spires and walls and windows; in South America, it was the high bell tower and the often pink-white plaster walls; in New England, it was the tall spire of the frame structure, the primitive, uncomfortable shape with white painted woodwork and clear glass windows facing on the village green.

Today the design is no longer so simple, so clear; it becomes modernistic free-form, parabolas arching against the Sunday morning sky; built with glass, steel and concrete, wholly new types of materials never dreamed of in the great Gothic cathedrals of the past.

Changes in church design and interior planning, contrary to the views of many who oppose the modern modes, are not the product of whims and fancies and a desire to keep up with the Joneses religiously. True, people like the modern, the up-to-date. We do not pray or worship better, or honor God and his gifts more worthily, by being uncomfortable or gazing on ugly and overdone mid-Victorian church architecture. Whether it is traditional or otherwise is not the question.

Rather, the church is asking: "Does it help in our worship of God? Does it add to or detract from the meaning of what we do and say here? Are the people of God who come here to worship together a part of the altar and the worship, or is there too great a separation in space? Is the Table of the Lord too far from the people who have come to share the Eucharist? Do the design and the shape and the whole intent of the architects meet the needs of this particular church, its funds, its character, its people? Do they serve to make their worship more immediate, more effective?"

In 1957 the Bureau of Church Building of the National Council of Churches and the Department of Architecture of Rensselaer Polytechnic Institute at Troy, New York, sponsored a conference on the topic "Building for Worship." The Rev. Edward S. Frey, director of the Lutheran Church's commission on architecture, addressed the meeting, delivering what is considered a historical statement on the whole meaning of the new architecture.

Success in building a church, Dr. Frey said, depends largely on where and how you begin; but it does not begin with architecture at all. "The congregation and the architect must first be concerned with *program* and not architecture. What is the purpose of the building they are to build? Who is He whom we worship, and what is worship? These are the questions that must be answered and the business of answering them is the first thing on the building program . . ."[1]

The building must take its pattern and shape out of liturgy, out of the concerns of those who come there to pray, out of the shape of need as it reaches out to the Father, to the sacred table around which the family of the Lord gathers.

Dr. Frey put his emphasis on meaning before all else. For instance, the question of where and how the church choir should be located is not decided on the basis of what will look well, but, rather, what is the purpose of the choir theologically, religiously, in the plan and meaning of worship.

What does the choir mean? Is it simply a group of expert singers providing an interlude in the business of worshiping God? Dr. Frey suggests: "The choir is a part of the service, a part of the congregation. Even though it may lead in the musical responses, even though it may offer hymns and music of its own, it is not an independent function of the service of worship, but an integral part of it."

In a manual prepared by the Lutheran Church's Commission on Church Architecture, there are procedures that Dr. Frey, as chairman, has set up.

---

[1] "The Role of Theology in Church Architecture," published in the *Pastor's Desk Book,* September, 1957, p. 1.

"Buildings for the use of the church are not ends in themselves," states the opening chapter. "They are tools in the hands of a congregation for the work of the Lord. Their plan and design must be reasoned in terms of the task they are to accomplish.

"Architecture is the business of the architect. Program is the business of the congregation. Much must be done by the congregation before drawings are made or any construction or remodeling is begun. Building committees often start at the wrong end of their task. They begin busily with the problems of architecture: What will the building look like? Where will it be placed on the site? How much will it cost? It is a waste of time to try to answer questions such as these at the very beginning of a building program. The congregation's first job is to write the program of its mission in the community. The architectural interpretation of this program then answers the question so often asked prematurely.

"By the word *program* as used in this manual, we mean everything the congregation does to express its faith and mission. The building facilities, whether they be old or new, must be made to serve the program. By the term *building program,* we mean everything the congregation does in pursuing the business at hand of making studies and decisions that will lead to adequate building facilities for its God-given task.

"If the work of the church for which building facilities are to be provided is understood and an effort made to write this out, the congregation's understanding of itself and its mission will be deepened and its chances of a successful building enterprise will be greatly enhanced. . . . Such questions as the following must be asked and answered:

"(1) Who are we as individuals? as a congregation? How many of us are there? Where are our ages, groupings, and individual needs? What does the congregation need to know about itself, its neighborhood, its mission?

"(2) In respect to the preceding questions, what rooms and equipment are believed to be necessary for the congregation's work? What is the 'servant role' of the church today? Do we have *sociological* responsibilities in regard to building?

"(3) How are we to worship in church? In Sunday church school? Will we change our present practice in corporate worship in any way?

"(4) What is the whole program in parish education, including teaching, study, fellowship, evangelism, pastoral and lay ministry, service? What new methods or curricula are to be used in Christian education? Which old ones are to be retained and which discarded?

"(5) What have we to say of the role of architecture and the fine arts in the service of our building enterprise?"[2]

The manual goes into detail regarding physical organization of committees, and activities, the plot plan, the floor plans, the elevations, spacing required or requested by the various heads of the church program, nursery, primary, social halls, costs and contracts, questions to be raised with the architect when this stage is reached, payment schedule programs, inspections, permits, fund-raising procedures, techniques, personnel, furniture, equipment, promotion.

But the heart of the whole plan is found in the committee on worship, which has to be a functioning part of the building program. Here is the *raison d'être* for all else that happens. "A well-designed church," the manual states, "shouts the belief of those who worship there."[3]

Much of the new designs, new art, and new concepts in church building have been subjected to criticism, occasionally razor-edged.

Some critics have actually complained that the church pro-

---

[2] *Manual for the Building Enterprise*, published by Commission on Church Architecture, Lutheran Church in America, New York, N.Y., 1965, pp. 10–11.
[3] *Ibid.*, p. 38.

vided too much in the way of "services" to the people. On the other hand, Claire Cox, a journalist who for years has written on religion for United Press International, points out in *The New Time Religion* that the elaborate new churches with stainless-steel kitchens, nurseries for children too young for Sunday school, and all the other "fringe benefits of organized faith" actually are serving important new roles in community responsibility. Declares Miss Cox:

"The churches are drawing more than just their members; they are serving entire neighborhoods around them. Local churches used to rely mainly on secular agencies for welfare, hospitals, and schools or had to depend on national groups for such good works. That no longer is true. Parish house programs are one evidence. Some churches have staffs of social workers, while bowling alleys and bingo tables are the answers to community need in other cases."[4]

The house of God is also the house of the people of God. And what is equally true, it serves the needs of worship. Modern architecture is no longer merely design and tradition. It is comfort, it is rest, it is acoustics, it is ritual made more meaningful by being closer to the people, so that each act of communal worship is accented, more fully grasped, more completely made a part of the congregation as it reaches out in song, in prayer, in listening, in the quiet itself. All of this is reflected in the new architecture and its role in the life of modern worship.

In the United Nations Building in New York City, there is an ultra-modern chapel for prayer. Because it was planned to meet the spiritual needs of many peoples, from all the world, Christians, Buddhists, Muslims, Indians, Jews, deists and nondeists, it was designed with none of the traditional symbols of traditional religions. No Cross, no Crescent, no Star of David. It is a room with a strange perspective, with a light so soft the room seems to

---

[4] Claire Cox, *The New Time Religion*. Englewood Cliffs, New Jersey: Prentice-Hall, 1961, p. 156.

reach into infinity. There is an abstract mural of bright colors at the far end. In the center of the room there is a single slab of stone presenting a rectangular flat frame on which a single light, its source hidden in the recesses of the shadowed ceiling, shines down.

Here all the world can worship together regardless of creed or lack of creed. Here each man is his own priest, interpreting the light and the shadows, even the liturgy of silence, as he understands them, the brotherhood not of one religion, but of a universe.

A short distance up the block from the United Nations, on East 47th Street, there is a Roman Catholic Church, built to accommodate not only members of the parish but also Catholics from all over the world who serve on the various U.N. delegations.

The Catholic church also is modern. The interior is singularly striking. It is quite simple. But the altar is dominated by a towering, massive figure of Jesus Christ. It is a Christ of great strength, looking out upon the congregation, upon the United Nations beyond, upon the world.

For God can be found in both the chapel and the church.

And equally in the world outside.

CHAPTER XV

BEYOND THE WALLS

In sum, the church of our day appears to be saying: We will reach out as far as the mind and soul can reach—to the very fringes of the infinite.

The church of the Middle Ages was everywhere in the world. It was the church of the multitudes on one side and the Medici on the other. It was the Holy Roman Empire, it touched every aspect of life. It was the church of politics and royal intrigue, of business and culture; it was, in effect, an active partner of the world, participating as the all-powerful voice of faith itself.

Following the Reformation and the assault on monasticism from many sides, through the intellectuals, through the French Revolution, through the new nineteenth-century science, the church retreated.

The church within the walls—formalistic, ritual-centered, translating every Biblical verse into absolutes—reached full flower in the Victorian era as an aftermath of the Puritan ethic, with its severe strictures against all manner of worldly activity. Post-puritanism accepted the strictures in form, if not in fact.

Religion became a Sunday morning in church. Outside the walls the role of the church was secondary to the hunger and greed of man.

In the second half of the twentieth century, as the churches draw closer in new ecumenical understanding, religion begins to reach out beyond the walls again to embrace the world outside and the universe beyond. Once again, awakening takes place not in rituals but in realities.

The briefly flaming "God is Dead" movement was not, in actual fact, a cry that God is dead but rather that the church which tried to imprison religion within the walls is dead. It died because it lacked relevance to so much the walls could not encompass.

The new church beyond the walls is not really a church at all, if we mean by this word an edifice. It is more properly the great *église* of humanity itself. Beyond the walls many also find Christ, on the streets, in the barrooms, in the gutters, in pain, in urban conflict, and in riot. Beyond the walls involves the whole renewal of religion, as old myths change and as new religious dimensions affirm that God is active here and not far off in the universe.

The Rev. Malcolm Boyd, whose iconoclastic role in modern prayer we discussed in an earlier chapter, prepared a special statement for this book, a moving statement from a priest of the lost and hurt and hungry, beyond the walls: "There are no boundaries beyond which we dare not move, for God is not limited by boundaries. God is with us always in the charted areas into which we move in Abrahamitic-Christological faith.

"Surely, this means we must have the courage to seek altogether new forms in which to express our interpretation of Christianity. Form without meaning is a dry, ugly, even blasphemous charade. Discontinuity between worship and real life (as a Jesuit friend of mine recently expressed it) is a lost enterprise. The demand of Christians in this generation is overwhelmingly in favor of honesty, and this means a radical departure from old forms which frequently possess cultural rather than Christian significance.

"I try to be a realist, too, and on that basis find our particular time in history to be one of immense hope. It is a time 'come of age'; it is a time when men have the very faith and hope and love to look, both within and outside themselves, for the reality of a 'religionless Christianity.' All things are made new; so we are presently caught up in the intensity and dynamics of actual ecumenism as well as an altogether new world view. We may have to redefine many supposedly basic concepts of 'the Faith'; yet Jesus is with us in the motivation and work of such very redefinition. We do not worship 'the Faith'; to do so would be idolatry. We worship only God, who, unlike our dogmas, rituals, ethics and even the Bible, is holy."

This is a statement that presents the Christ not in statues, paintings, remoteness, but in the immediacy of all our lives.

It is the Christ one finds in the moment of tawdry little night spots, against saxophone and brass drums; the Christ who serves in the East Harlem Protestant parish; the Christ of Father Flanagan's Boys Town; the Christ of the Roman Catholic "Little Sisters of Jesus" who serve others but never preach and who live with the joy of service in their eyes.

It is also the Christ found in the following words:

"Human dignity, human freedom, and the noble speak of building the earth: the time has passed when Catholics might speak of these as merely human, merely secular ideals. The Church has made her attitude unambiguously clear; they are authentically Christian values. But in taking this stand, the Church has also proven her capacity to learn; she has learned from modern and contemporary man's experience.

"But more particularly, she has learned from that school to which the contemporary world owes so much: the American experience. For without the American democratic experiment, dedicated to the proposition that 'all men are created equal' and 'endowed by their Creator with certain inalienable rights,' how much longer would it have taken the world—and the Church—to recognize how sacred and central these rights must be, not only to the developed human sense, but to the Christian sense as well? Without the American experience of religious pluralism, how much longer would we have had to wait for the recent Council's Constitution on Religious Liberty?"[1]

Such a statement as this, one might almost imagine to be the work of a liberal Protestant. In fact, it is an excerpt from a speech made by Father Pedro Arrupe, S.J., Father General of the Jesuits, at Fordham University on April 5, 1966.

Here, as another instance, is a statement from a report of the Lutheran Church on "The Church in Social Welfare":

"The new life in Christ manifests itself in the same total concern which Christ manifested for the whole man in all his need and for all men regardless of worth. Whether the Christian actually speaks the word of forgiveness or simply in love accepts the sinner as he is, whether he gives the cup of cold water in Jesus's name, or renders some other needed aid, depends upon the particular time and place. One form of aid must not be subordinated to the other . . .

"This does not mean that the Christian social worker must preach a sermon to his client or hold a prayer meeting in his office. It does mean that he may (indeed must) in his own way and in his own language proclaim Christ. For what transpires between worker and client—regardless of the specific content of the act—must also express the reconciling love of the Father. The material or professional help that is given must be given without the ulterior motive of winning the client for the church, but simply to meet his need in love. Neither should the gospel be preached to him merely as a means toward bettering his material

---

[1] Father Pedro Arrupe, S.J., "News and Views," *Commonweal*, Vol. LXXXIV, No. 5, April 22, 1966, p. 140.

and physical condition. The need of the moment must decide what Christian love is constrained to do. . . ."[2]

Christian love led in San Francisco to the formation of a committee, which was the beginning of a mission of the church to homosexuals. Its membership included representatives of homosexual organizations, including the Daughters of Belitis and the Mattachine Society, and of Christian churches including the Lutheran, Methodist, Protestant Episcopal, United Church of Christ and the National Council of Churches. The work of this organization did much to dispel the misunderstandings that have made it so difficult for church people to understand or work with homosexuals at all. These homosexuals have indeed been in large measure spiritual pariahs, outcasts by reason of what they are, voluntarily or involuntarily.

Does the church belong in an area like this? Some churchgoers assert that religion has no business with such groups, that homosexuals are the business of the physicians, psychiatrists, psychologists. "The homosexual is sick—physically, emotionally, morally, sexually; I consider homosexuality revolting," said a business executive who is a strong supporter of his church and a firm believer in "born again" Christianity. Sincere in his beliefs, he finds it difficult to comprehend those who seek to make the church more Christlike in its dealings with the homosexual problem.

But others ask: Is not this where Christ is to be found— among the despairing, the rejected, the despaired of?

The homosexual world is one of the places where it requires an extra bit of courage to stand up and say, "Yes, Lord. He also is Your child, and my brother."

Nor can one avoid, in discussing the church of our times, areas where social-action religion has moved decisively, effectually, into the front lines—in Selma, in Little Rock, on a hun-

---

[2] *The Church in Social Welfare*, Lutheran Church in America, 1964, p. 36.

dred picket lines for people deprived of their rights not only as citizens but as human beings.

Today there are many special ministries of the church to the world: ministries to migrant workers, to the night people of our great cities, to the dope addicts, to the prostitutes, to the girls crowded into women's jails, to housing projects, to supermarkets, to leper colonies and to street gangs. Such ministries are truly a new way of going forth into all the world. They are a ministry of clergy in some instances, laity in others. It is a specialization in mission, an expertise in concern.

The role of the National Council of Churches offers a glimpse of the many aspects of this church-beyond-the-church, for all major Protestant churches participate, and now the Roman Catholics cooperate with the council. (Roman Catholics' social efforts in many areas parallel and often go beyond that of Protestant churches in service.) The National Council has ministries that reach out to the whole world in need through what is called the Church World Service. Thousands of participating churches of all denominations participate in this program, providing millions of dollars in materials, clothes, food, implements for work programs and projects, money, and effort—to go to hungry, ill-fed, war-whipped, flood-ravaged peoples of the world. An army of church workers reaches out with aid to literally millions of human beings. This, too, is Christ beyond the walls.

The Council reaches out to the sick, the hospitalized, the mentally ill, the drug addict, the prisoner in jail; to labor and management problems; to race relations; to poverty programs and rehabilitation programs for sick people. Much criticized, sometimes denounced, the Council has had the courage to stand its ground, in conscience, in action beyond the immobile walls.

We move from one dimension to the next, and we return again to that place where two or three are gathered. There is much about the mystical and its meanings that we can study and discuss and experience in the church within the walls, for this is the comradeship, this is the communion, this is the breaking of the bread. And Christ is there with us.

It is surprising for some to meet Him outside the places of worship. It is new to meet Him in the whirl of the factory, the bustle of the supermarket, the shouting of pickets, and among the thieves, harlots, protesters, demonstrators, atheists. But He is there with all of these in the unseen edifice of human need.

CHAPTER XVI

UNSEEN HORIZONS

The question becomes, in essence: How valid, how durable, are these new directions of the church in their main thrust?

Few in religion today question the need for change in the church as in all else, change in standards, in attitudes, in approaches, in ritual, in liturgy. The absolutes and simplistics of the primitive peoples of three thousand or more years past—or even three hundred—cannot always meet the complexities and ambiguities of today. The debate arises not on the reality of the need but on the character of response the church should make.

At the outset, this survey of what is happening, and what directions are developing, indicates that the modern church's response to the hungers, the suffering, the needs of the world is producing changes of a fundamental nature in theological ideas, in long-held absolutes, and in interpretation of good and evil.

We discover that the new "situation ethics" modifies the stone-tablet absolutism of the Ten Commandments. We discover that churchmen who support and promote this situational approach to right and wrong make full use of the time-honored slogan that circumstances alter cases—even when they may involve abortion, premarital or extramarital sex, even deliberate violation of the law, as in states where birth control is illegal but clergymen nevertheless advise their people to employ contraceptive methods.

Does this mean that the church has abandoned all its previously held morality in favor of a pot-pourri of modern moral experimentation? Certainly not from what is indicated. The overall picture is of a church reacting with a gradual adaptation of what appears good. Psychiatry, psychology, and many aspects of psychoanalysis—once subjects of vigorous denunciation—are now tools of the church, utilized by pastors and their aids. It is true that these disciplines, employed in conjunction with religion, are minimizing more and more the role of fear and guilt in religion and church life. The churches have not, of course, eliminated guilt or sin from their concern; but these negative forces no longer play a dominant role in the religion based on the love and compassion of Christ.

Guilt, however, and sin or imagined sin, do play a basic role in spiritual or religious therapy, and often in the church this aspect is explored in close cooperation with psychology and psychiatry. The church does not abandon a metaphysical position in healing; rather, in modern terms, it orients that role to the broad concept that much of our sickness—physical, mental, and emotional—is brought upon us by our own hatreds and prejudices, our need for vengeance, our need to hurt others.

In a guilt-haunted modern world, much of religion has learned to work with medical and psychological disciplines in a team program of help. It is a teamwork of worldly disciplines and religions; it accepts and strives to understand the healing force that seems to act in both supernatural and natural ways.

Sin, guilt, sickness, health, and their interrelated meanings, in a new church with a new orientation in which sin is not only individual but also social—all of this is involved in the changing patterns of church life and attitudes. All becomes part of the interrelated concerns of religion involved not only with the importance of the life beyond this life, but also with the importance of life here and now. This is why there are new patterns in sin and guilt and the nature of the responsibilities and moral demands Christianity places upon mankind in *this* world.

Yet changes involve not only social action. They are also personal, immediate; they involve nature—and supernature. How in modern times do we communicate our needs; to whom and to what do we pray? In what words, in what terms? This too, we find, is a part of the change, of the new outreach, in both Protestant and Catholic rituals and liturgy. The church seeks to sweep out the false and meaningless; the comfortable repetitions, the empty language found often in outdated prayer, the entreating of God to pour down his punishment on our enemies. The new prayer is no longer bombast and rolling phrases. It becomes the simple words of our deepest personal meaning. It is the people of God and of this new church reaching out to reality.

Not everything that happens in this new movement is reassuring and comfortable. The whole glossolalia movement, the spread of speaking in tongues, raises many questions. It is possible that man may be able to communicate with the infinite in emotion-based sounds rather than intellectual words; it is possible that glossolalia is truly a language of the Holy Spirit. But there remain serious doubts. This is true also of some of the new music, the liturgical developments, the hill-billy hysteria that many believe approaches the tamborine tent shows in its underlying emotional appeal.

Yet even here, in murky areas, these are questions rather than attacks, they are doubts, probings, part of modern man's search. In large measure this is true also of the extrasensory activities and the need for more knowledge and greater understanding of ESP and its religious implications, of prophecy and demonology, witchcraft and possession; of the church's attitude toward spiritualism, toward the new drugs that some consider to be dehydrated demons in pill form.

These are areas in which there is increased activity and interest, in the confused and contradictory patterns of our age. The church finds itself involved in reexamination of its own long-held positions on many of these topics. And because men still turn for guidance to their religious leaders, religion becomes even more deeply involved in what is happening in these supernatural and semi-supernatural areas.

The churches, as we have seen, are beginning to make cautious reexamination of their theological positions in such fields, and changes are emerging in official attitudes in some cases, as for example, the position of the Lutherans on glossolalia and the Presbyterian position on religious therapy in the churches.

We live in a cosmos of change. Man changes, often more quickly and radically than his institutions. Moral and social codes change. The person living by today's accepted codes will find little help in theology that is no longer applicable to the problems of daily life.

Change is the very essence also of the church itself, because it *is* the people of God. As they unfold in their lives, so does the church; as they reach out in need, so does the church; as they accept, as they probe, as they take on the burden of the world, so does the church.

The new changing church is the Living Church—it is the people, the world in renewal, breathing the breath of change which is itself the gift of God.

INDEX

A

Abortion, 6, 32, 35–36
Academy of Religion and Mental Health, 24, 27, 29
Adler, Alfred, 23
Agape, 3
Allen, the Rev. Michael, 68–69
American Foundation of Religion and Psychiatry, 27
American Medical Association, *Journal* of, 121
American Society of Psychic Research, 77
Anderson, the Rev. George C., quoted, 24
Arrupe, Father Pedro, quoted, 132–133
Astrology, 87
Atheism, 1, 69

B

Baptism, 3, 51–52, 54–55, 96
Baptists, 3
Barth, Karl, 92
Bartlett, the Very Rev. C. Julian, quoted, 63
Beatles, the, 47
Bennett, Father Dennis, 50, 52
Bible, the, interpretation of, 2–3, 12, 21–22
    New Standard, 7
    and speaking in tongues, 52–53
    (*See also* New Testament)
Birth control, 6, 35–36
Blanton, Smiley, 27
Bloy, the Rt. Rev. Francis Eric, 50
Bonhoeffer, Dietrich, 29, 44, 92
    quoted, 94